Design and Technology
in Primary School Classrooms

Design and Technology in Primary School Classrooms: Developing teachers' perspectives and practices

Edited by
Les Tickle

 The Falmer Press
(A member of the Taylor & Francis Group)
London · New York · Philadelphia

UK   The Falmer Press, Falmer House, Barcombe, Lewes,
East Sussex, BN8 5DL

USA   The Falmer Press, Taylor & Francis Inc., 1900 Frost Road, Suite
101, Bristol, PA 19007

Selection and editorial material
©copyright L. Tickle 1990

First published in 1990
British Library Cataloguing in Publication Data

Design and technology in primary school classrooms: developing
teachers' perspectives and practices.
    1. Primary schools. Curriculum subjects: Design and technology.
Teaching
I. Tickle, Les
372.3'5

ISBN 1-85000-582-6

Library of Congress Cataloguing-in-Publication Data available on
request

Typeset in 11/13 Bembo by
Chapterhouse, The Cloisters, Formby L37 3PX

Printed in Hong Kong by Imago

Contents

Design the activity of identifying, investigating, and analyzing problems, proposing ideas and solutions, and implementing and evaluating the proposals by bringing ideas and materials to bear on the problem.

Technology the knowledge (and the application of knowledge) of the properties of materials and concepts of functions, processes and phenomena, which can provide solutions to and control over environmental and technical problems.

List of Contributors

Mark Devereux teachers at Elm Tree Middle School, Lowestoft, Suffolk.

Sally Frost is deputy headteacher at Sidegate Primary School, Ipswich, Suffolk.

Mark Lancaster teaches at William Cowper Junior and Infant School, Newtown, Birmingham.

Eric Marshall teaches at Fairfield Junior School, Stockton, Cleveland.

Alan Rosenberg teaches at St James Junior School, Kings Lynn, Norfolk.

Adrian Scargill is headteacher at Aldborough County Primary School, Norfolk.

Elisabeth Thompson is headteacher at Bucklesham County Primary School, Suffolk.

Les Tickle is a senior lecturer in the School of Education, University of East Anglia.

Chapter 1

Introduction

Les Tickle

> We should find ways of introducing all primary pupils . . . of all abilities (male and female) to the activities of designing and making, in ways which will not be intimidating to primary school teachers but will build naturally on the strong tradition of practical work in primary schools. — Sir Keith Joseph (EM and YFA, 1985).

When Sir Keith Joseph made this observation he was acknowledging the value of the kinds of learning experiences represented in an exhibition of schools' projects. The exhibition had the title *Designing and Making* and represented those activities which also become known as Craft, Design and Technology (EM and YFA, 1985) and now, Design and Technology (DES 1988b; 1989). In giving a seal of approval the then Secretary of State for Education and Science was joining a long line of support amongst educators and politicians for the use of practical, problem-solving activities as a mode of learning. He was also asserting the value of what had come to be seen in recent years as a different content in those activities, compared with conventional practical work in primary schools.

To claim that practice in primary school classrooms had been influenced by the development of practical activities to the extent that they had become a strong tradition, however, was a bold claim. Indeed it is curious, if such a tradition is widespread in practice, that it should be necessary to suggest that primary school teachers might be intimidated by designing and making activities. The evidence is, of course, that there is no such widespread, established strength in the primary school curriculum. That is not to say that practical work does not occur. But it is clear from a variety of evidence (which will be considered later in this book) that there is a clear need for it to be more widely developed. The range of skills, knowledge and attitudes which primary pupils experience is still dominated by the elementary school traditions of teaching the 'basics'. Over-concentration on the practice of basic skills in literacy and numeracy was recently identified by the Department of Education and Science (DES, 1985). Not only the content but also the teaching methods of primary schools conform for the most part to 'traditional' approaches.

Yet these have not been the only approaches, as the variety of curriculum in some English primary schools shows. Support for a broad curriculum in a range of academic subjects has been considerable. The values of child-centred teaching have also taken hold to some extent. Thus there have been alignments among teachers and others to particular beliefs about primary education. Often a set of conflicting beliefs coexists side by side (Blyth, 1965; Berlak and Berlak, 1981). Usually within those beliefs the value of practical activities has sought recognition and legitimacy, either for their worth as a means of educating (Read, 1943) or as having intrinsic value in their own right (Ross, 1978).

Tensions and stresses in the primary school curriculum between the elementary tradition of teaching literacy and numeracy, the academic view of school subjects in preparation for secondary education, and approaches to learning characterized by first-hand, individualized, practical experiences (Blyth, 1965) continue to vie for 'legitimate' places. Amid these already existing tensions there has been a recent and rather sudden renewed recognition of the economic value to the nation of knowledge in the area of craft, design and technology. The developments of new high-technology industries and the importance placed on competitive, creative product renewal have spurred that recognition. Demands for a more 'relevant' curriculum linked directly to the industrial economy at all stages of formal education have thus grown. Expressions of this 'utilitarian' view of the curriculum are now being implanted in primary schools. Technology is part of the national curriculum.

With the new demands, it seems, there is a need to build new traditions, or to strengthen elements of older ones which failed to establish a lasting place in classroom practice. In this instance, design and technology, that 'tradition' is to be built of a combination of scientific and technological understanding, coupled with the intellectual qualities, practical know-how, and aesthetic sensitivities of designing and making artefacts. Sir Keith Joseph recognized that the knowledge, skills and attitudes of primary school teachers are key factors in the process of establishing such a new tradition. Change of any kind may be threatening for many of these teachers. Design and technology seems particularly intimidating to some because it requires de-skilling from well-proven teaching methods. There are different classroom management techniques needed for its activities. It demands new learning of concepts as a basis for instruction. These have to be achieved while maintaining a firm grip on the successes of past practices, and against pressure for improvements in 'standards' of literacy and numeracy.

Sir Keith Joseph, I believe, was seeking a foundation on which to build new practices by turning to the art and craft work of primary schools. He might, in addition, have sought to build upon the foundation of professionalism which many teachers bring to those schools. That is a professionalism in which continuous, career-long learning takes place. There is a constant search to improve knowledge, skills and attitudes as a basis for successful and effective teaching. These changes in teachers' knowledge enable curriculum change to occur. Those who adhere to such professionalism accept the intimidating, and live with the intrinsic uncertainties of learning.

That 'tradition', like the practical work to which Sir Keith Joseph referred, is not yet completely established either. There have been many advances in recent years in the movement towards openly examining and improving classroom practices. Those advances have been made by teachers concerned to improve practice through self-reflection and classroom research. Through such studies the development of perspectives and practice can advance beyond anything recognizable in Sir Keith Joseph's appeal. Indeed the openness to learning which teacher-research demonstrates *is* a way of introducing all primary pupils to the activities of designing and making. What is needed first is a way to generate and spread that openness among teachers, coupled with a commitment by government, local education authorities, and governors of schools to adequately resource craft, design and technology.

In this book I have sought to bring together a summary of the state of design and technology in primary schools, in the context of the development of a national curriculum. I have tried to convey the uncertainties and debates about the nature of design and technology, which are reflected even in the changes of title – from CDT, to designing and making, to technology, and design and technology. In the light of the way the subject is commonly referred to in schools, I have used the shorthand term CDT in discussion. Like its label, its emergence is characterized by conflict, compromise and curriculum growing-pains. Those uncertainties may demonstrate to teachers who find the subject threatening that even the 'experts' are learning. This summary will provide a basis for understanding CDT in the primary school curriculum. The development of teachers' perspectives is thus approached initially through a *curriculum* perspective, identifying the educational aims of CDT, and placing those aims within a broader picture of recent developments in education. At the same time, the book presents the central features of the subject's content and associated teaching methods. The curriculum aims of CDT are combined with a *subject* perspective in which the essential features of knowledge content and learning process are outlined. The importance of that content, and the nature of the design process, for classroom management provide the need also for a *teaching strategies* perspective. That is provided partly through examples of projects undertaken by teachers themselves, showing how they developed their own knowledge, skills, understanding, and capacities for engaging in problem-solving. In addition, a proposal for a series of lessons devised by a teacher illustrates detailed teaching strategies. Those examples are followed by a series of studies of classroom events and accounts of teachers' thinking about them. These studies illustrate further the kinds of teaching strategies adopted in CDT projects. They also offer a *professional development* perspective, showing how the study of events in classrooms can lead to improved understanding of teaching and learning, and to changes in practice where change is appropriate.

The curriculum perspective will enable teachers and student teachers to place recent developments in CDT in a national context, by illustrating how it has emerged and the forms it is taking. It also shows how those developments have occurred across the age phases of education, so that conceptions of primary school CDT can be related to what is happening in secondary schools. In both cases this perspective identifies how the curriculum is shaped by the values and actions of people and groups who are influential in its making. In schools, teachers are influential in that process of change, and the development of CDT in primary schools can be enhanced by a clear perspective of its place in the curriculum.

Understanding and belief in teachers' practical knowledge often stem from a commitment to subject knowledge. In primary education that is usually combined with a view of how children learn *through* a particular activity or subject. The subject perspective in the case of CDT is based first and foremost upon the nature of the activity of designing and making. That is combined with specific content — a marriage of know-how and know-what. While the curriculum perspective opens the way for subject knowledge, the development of specific processes and content is illustrated in examples of work done by Mike Lancaster and Mark Devereux, as part of their introduction to both learning and teaching CDT. These are far from exhaustive of the content of CDT. Rather, they indicate how, through practical projects which are adaptable for school use, 'manageable' elements of subject knowledge can be built. In these examples the problem-solving process combines with knowledge of materials and use of tools, which are enhanced by knowledge of mechanisms and of energy.

Teaching strategies appropriate to the character and quality of CDT also need to be developed. These require a combination of instruction, guided discovery and problem-solving, used appropriately for different purposes. In Eric Marshall's example, a project on structures and forces, the effective transmission of knowledge, skills and attitudes is determined by considerable teacher direction and guidance. The work also incorporates guided discovery and problem-solving activities, illustrating how a range of strategies can be adopted for specific purposes.

The studies of classroom events made by teachers provide detailed illustrations of how practices have been implemented and evaluated. They bring together, each in a different way, the curriculum, subject, teaching strategies and professional perspectives associated with the introduction and development of CDT in primary school classrooms.

Adrian Scargill describes the tentative beginning of CDT in a small ill-equipped rural school. The initiative of the headteacher, stemming from her own evaluation of the curriculum, together with the influence of television, the support of an advisory teacher, and cooperation with other schools in the same rural locality, got problem-solving activities off the ground. This was followed by extending opportunities to other children in the school. The limits of that extension are clear and severe. Yet they were tackled with a view of the importance of progression and continuity in the curriculum planning of the school. The place of CDT within 'integrated' topic-based study was also an issue in the school, highlighting a tension between the need for flexibility and an equitable sharing of limited practical facilities. The study also shows how the introduction of CDT, after a short time, raised issues among the teachers about the classroom experiences of the children. Those experiences are evaluated in the study, which asks many questions. It is in the search for evidence which may substantiate or refute the implied, speculative judgments which follow from those questions that a better perspective on CDT and its associated teaching methods will be found.

A more detailed and focused view of one aspect of classroom experience — the nature of independent learning — and a group of twelve 10- to-11-year-old pupils' responses to it, is written by Sally Frost. The situation is one where designing and making and technological activities are a well-established part of the curriculum. Some of the values which underlie the work are set out in 'principles of procedure' which help to establish a 'process' approach to curriculum practice, and to achieve the aim of independent learning — or so it was believed. However, this group study shows that while four children respond favourably, in the teachers' terms, to the conditions established to achieve that aim, eight do not. In particular the nature of risks involved in problem-solving were disconcerting, raising anxieties amongst these pupils. They preferred to be told what to do. What is more, this chapter shows how risk-taking and decision-making are avoided by some children, sometimes by 'latching on' to pupils who they deem to be good and conducting menial tasks for them. The part played by some pupils in determining the kinds of experiences of others are an important highlight of this study. From the teacher's immediate perspective, however, it is the dilemmas inherent in teaching which are illuminated here — showing that the central aims of CDT carry with them considerable potential for uncertainty and anxiety on the part of teachers. Opening up these dilemmas will need to be a feature of the developing perspective on primary school CDT.

Elisabeth Thompson's study into individuality and originality in the conduct of 7-year-old pupils' designing helps to display her dilemmas as she 'thinks through' the events observed and her own contrived and preferred responses to the children. Contrasting and competing values in educational thought set the context for the elaboration of tensions as they affect the author directly, in both her 'usual' and her research stances. These values, about the ownership of knowledge and the relationships between teachers and pupils, and the issues of curriculum transmission which they underlie, are an intrinsic element of CDT. Questions of choice, decision-making, initiative, independence, and power are central to these issues. This study concludes with clear judgments about teaching methods. For this teacher what seemed like competing beliefs about the best way to encourage pupils' learning became complementary. The nature, place, and value of instruction was 'redeemed' through careful analysis of events, to coexist in teaching strategies with 'freer', problem-posing ones.

Alan Rosenberg's account of the degree of choice and cooperation which existed during a group activity among 7-year-old pupils addresses two other issues which are central to CDT teaching. He shows how the pupils reconcile the demands which he, as teacher, makes upon them with the opportunity he offers for them to make decisions for themselves. The study also demonstrates the considerable sophistication of young children in the organization of a cooperative venture. In respect of both choice and cooperation, Alan Rosenberg reveals how his own ideals were constrained by his actions as a teacher.

In curriculum perspectives on primary education questions of choice, freedom, child-centredness, independence, cooperation, discovery-learning, and so on, abound. The relationships between content and learning process, between teacher and pupils, are in perpetual debate. In the work which follows those themes recur. While defining them as issues which are brought to the surface by CDT, it will be clear that they are not confined to it. By developing perspectives on CDT and appropriate teaching methods which would represent its essential qualities and characteristics, it will certainly be possible to consider and to understand the nature of the primary curriculum into which CDT is expected to fit.

References

BERLAK, A., and BERLAK, H. (1981) *Dilemmas of Schooling*, London, Methuen.

BLYTH, W. A. L. (1965) *English Primary Education: A Sociological Description*, London, Routledge and Kegan Paul.

DEPARTMENT OF EDUCATION AND SCIENCE (1985) *Better Schools*, London, HMSO.

EM AND YFA (East Midlands and Yorkshire Forum of Advisers in CDT) (1985) *Designing and Making: Learning Through Craft Design and Technology*, Wetherby, EM and YFA.

READ, H. (1943) *Education Through Art*, London, Faber.

ROSS, M. (1978) *The Creative Arts*, London, Heinemann.

Chapter 2

The Primary School Curriculum and Design and Technology

Les Tickle

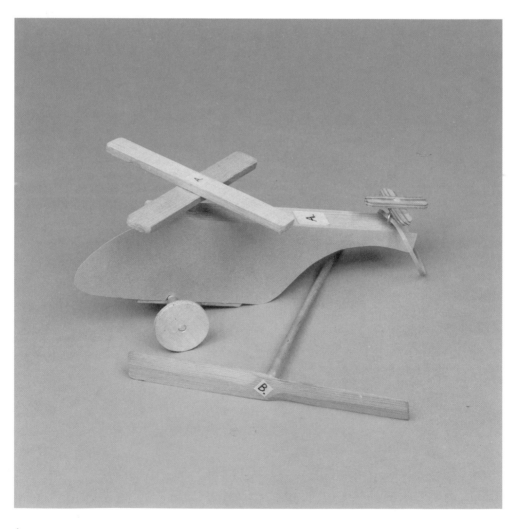

Government policy and legislation for the implementation of a national curriculum for state primary schools in England and Wales is now well known. Among other things, the Education Reform Act is intended to ensure that for pupils between the ages of 5 and 11 all schools will provide the same breadth and balance of curriculum subjects. Centred on the core subjects of English, mathematics and science, there will also be foundation subjects of technology, art, history, geography, music, and physical education. Religious education will also be required by law. It is expected that time will also be available for 'other popular subjects' and that curriculum content such as health education and information technology will be developed within the core and foundation subjects.

Defining the content of each of the core and foundation subjects is the responsibility of the National Curriculum Council (NCC). The detailed work is done by subject groups established for the specific purpose of deciding programmes of study, attainment targets, and assessment arrangements for pupils at different stages of schooling. These stages are defined as Key Stages 1 (5-to-7-year-olds), 2 (7-to-11-year-olds), 3 (11-to-14-year-olds) and 4 (14-to-16-year-olds). In the case of primary school technology, recommendations have come from two NCC subject working groups — Science, and Design and Technology. Their proposals amount to the implementation of new activities in most primary schools. There are no traditions or conventional practices associated with the 'new' subject of technology. Yet under the alternative title of craft, design and technology there had emerged some new activities in some schools. That happened very recently, and at a rapid pace. As we shall see in the next chapter, the nature of technology as a primary school subject defined by the NCC corresponds closely to curriculum practices which emerged within the more comprehensive (and more representative) title of craft, design and technology.

The place of CDT in policy relating to the primary curriculum was first evident from its inclusion in *The curriculum from 5 to 16* (DES, 1985b, para. 33). It had not previously been included in documents of curriculum policy. Now, we were advised, the curriculum of all schools should involve pupils in areas of learning which include aesthetic, creative, and technological experience. In the same year, the government white paper *Better Schools* set out formal policy for a broad, balanced and relevant curriculum aimed at ensuring a high quality of education for all pupils. It includes in its conception of the primary curriculum opportunities for 'craft and practical work leading up to some experience of design and technology and of solving problems' (DES, 1985a, para. 61). Such opportunities, it asserts, should be provided throughout the phase of primary education.

After these general statements of policy were made, with some brief indications of what CDT might entail, the publication of guidelines from Her Majesty's Inspectors relating to primary school CDT was awaited. They were provided in the 'Curriculum Matters' paper number nine, *Craft, design and technology from 5–16* (DES, 1987a). Although it is called a discussion document, it aims to set out a framework for schools to develop their CDT programmes. Furthermore, it is significant that this ninth discussion paper from HMI was the first to be published since the Government's intention to legislate for a national curriculum, and to establish a National Curriculum Council, was announced. It is, significantly, the first HMI discussion document explicitly intended to contribute to the work of the National Curriculum Council and its subject working groups, by defining a framework for teaching CDT throughout compulsory schooling.

In relation to the primary age range this document sets out in detail the aims and objectives of the subject in terms of activities in which all pupils should have taken part by the age of 11. It also sets out in some detail teaching and learning strategies, plans for achieving curriculum 'progression', and assessment procedures for the subject. In doing so it is the first detailed policy statement of the way the subject is regarded in relation to younger children. Those details will be discussed further in the next chapter.

The recency of such policies is evident from the fact that these aspects of curriculum were not included in earlier documents in anything like the same way, if at all. What is more, they were clearly not an active part of the primary school curriculum. Evidence provided by HMI, as well as research on primary education, shows that until very recently the activities related to CDT did not occur.

For example, *Primary Education in England* (DES, 1978) reported that studies relating to man-made artefacts, mechanical actions and physical sciences were comparatively rare in the representative sample of schools surveyed. Three-dimensional construction work was also 'not well developed'. The report called for opportunities for pupils to work with wood and other resistant materials and to learn to handle the tools and techniques associated with them. Concern was expressed in the Primary Survey about the lack of development of science education, within which many of the activities which are now regarded as CDT have developed.

With regard to very young children *Education 5–9* reiterated in relation to first schools the findings of the Primary Survey (DES, 1982, para. 2.143). CDT was still not an identifiable label and it was said by HMI that only occasionally or rarely were children found using a range of materials and tools. There was a general concern for the lack of what more recently became defined in policy as the processes of making, inventing, designing, and problem-solving.

For those children of the upper primary phase who were being educated in 8–12 middle schools in the early 1980s there was evidence of rather more provision of those kinds of activities. *Education 8–12* reported that twenty-five of the forty-nine schools surveyed provided craft, design and technology as an identifiable part of the curriculum (DES, 1985c, paras 2.95–2.103). This probably resulted from the attempts which had been made by some middle schools to provide, at least for their older pupils, a transition into the kind of education provided in secondary schools. The quality of practice, however, was reported to be weak, with insufficient opportunities to experiment with materials, to produce individual solutions to problems, or to use imagination. Decision-making was severely restricted, and the opportunity to explore design possibilities rarely utilized. Furthermore, the variety of manipulative skills used by children was said by HMI to be insufficiently developed.

Even in 9–13 middle schools, where the provision of facilities and specialist teachers of CDT was much greater, HMI showed that it was carried out mostly with older pupils who, in a two-tier system, would be in secondary schools (DES, 1983, paras 7.100–7.103). Rarely did the pupils of conventional primary school age gain access to experiences of the designing and making kind. Even with the older pupils work was restricted largely to the acquisition and practice of basic manipulative skills, with limits on the extent of problem-solving and design decision-making.

The concern of HMI about the limited range of practical work, within which there was a concentration on didactic teaching methods, was reflected in more recent policy relating to both content and methods in primary education. *Better Schools* comments on the negative residual impact of the widespread concentration on basic skills in literacy and numeracy, unrelated to meaningful contexts and the application of the skills. It asserts that literacy and numeracy would benefit from the provision for children of greater opportunities to engage in scientific, practical and aesthetic activities. There is little doubt that this policy is derived from evidence claiming that a majority of schools over-concentrate their efforts on practice in, rather than application of, basic skills. It also claims that

> In about half of all classes much work in classrooms is so closely directed by the teacher that there is little opportunity either for oral discussion or for posing and solving practical problems. (DES, 1985a, para. 19).

Unlike the reports on middle schools, these claims about primary schools do not refer specifically to CDT. They maintain a broader picture of the primary curriculum than one defined only according to subjects. But they also emerged before the label of CDT had come to be attached to problem-solving activities in schools. In a survey of 285 primary schools carried out by HMI between 1982 and 1985, in which a subject analysis was backed by data, CDT was not included in the survey questions (Highfield, 1987). Seemingly it had not entered the consciousness of the primary schools Inspectorate (nor perhaps that of teachers) at that stage. It is only very recently that it has come to be seen as a 'subject', and even now some argue that it should not be so narrowly labelled.

The picture of craft, design and technology in primary classroom practice until very recent years is therefore consistently one of underdevelopment in terms of curriculum content and in relation to teaching and learning strategies. That view is supported by the evidence of the nature of primary curriculum practice in general (Bennett, 1976; Galton *et al.*, 1980; Boydell, 1981).

This picture does not mean that there have been no developments in the practice of problem-solving activities in individual primary school classrooms. Enterprising teachers, enthusiastic advisers, and energetic teacher educators have made some mark (Evans, undated; EM and YFA, 1985; Jinks, 1984; Shallcross, 1983; Schools Council, 1974; Williams, 1982; Williams and Jinks, 1985). Even so, the aspirations of recent policy are clearly a long way from being realized. However, there is now a sense that action is taking place on a wide scale.

The implementation by the Department of Trade and Industry of a national curriculum development project, *Problem Solving 5–13*, is evidence of official interest (Sellwood, 1987). It also indicates the source of that interest, the new industry-related influences upon schools. The Design Council, too, has taken a major stand on the importance of design-related activities in primary schools. Not only has it presented a widely publicized report, it has also launched its own termly *Big Paper* as a stimulus and resource for teachers (Design Council, 1987a and 1987b).

A plethora of activity in the production of guidelines for school practice by local education authorities, and in curriculum policy-making within individual schools, has also occurred in recent years. This has been supported by the production of video films and other materials for in-service teacher education, and for classroom use, by government departments, LEAs and commercial producers (DTI, 1987; CFL Vision, 1986; Kent TV, 1986).

Developments in classrooms practice in some primary schools, introducing CDT as a regular feature of their curriculum, is also occurring. Others are now anticipating the requirements of the national curriculum, trying to respond to the perceived pace of national developments in primary school CDT. The potential for a sudden surge of demand for curriculum development support and resources, when the Education Reform Act is fully implemented, is considerable.

Technology for 5-to-11-year-olds was included within the proposals of the NCC subject working group for science, giving it urgent consideration alongside the core subjects of the national curriculum. The proposals acknowledge that while technology is a growing area of the primary school curriculum, it has not yet begun in many primary classrooms (DES, 1988a, para. 5.6). In July 1988 the remit of the design and technology working group, which had been established to consider technology for the third and fourth key stages, was extended to include advice on primary technology (DES, 1988b). The final report of the design and technology working group and the statutory orders within the Education Reform Act which follow it, will ensure that CDT (in a particular form) is implemented in primary schools. It is clear that the Secretary of State intends that activities should begin with some urgency, with the implementation of attainment targets and national assessment and testing in technology by Autumn 1990 for 5- to-7-year-old pupils, and by Autumn 1991 for 8-to-11-year-olds (TES, 1988).

The national curriculum subject working groups provide the basis for attainment targets, overall content, knowledge, skills, and processes. These are discussed fully in the following chapter. However, the programmes of study will require teachers to determine the detail of those aspects of the subject, and the teaching approaches and organization best suited to the needs of pupils. In particular, we are told, the programmes of study will be written so as to accommodate the enterprise of teachers so that they may try out and develop new approaches (DES, 1987b, para. 27). In the case of CDT as a new feature of the primary school curriculum, that would presumably only happen with the provision of support which could help the teachers to gain initial competences, and then examine their practical experience of teaching CDT in normal classroom circumstances. Such in-school, in-service education, centred on the practical nature of the subject, will be a prerequisite to finding ways of introducing CDT to primary children without intimidating primary school teachers. Such teachers will need the *learning* support of colleagues and in-service tutors to provide them with the means of developing competences and exploring their own classroom practice, of learning from their innovation, and of further developing the content and teaching strategies in the longer term more autonomously.

References

BENNETT, N. (1976) *Teaching Styles and Pupil Progress*, London, Open Books.

BOYDELL, D. (1981) 'Classroom Organization 1970–77', in Simon, B., and Willcocks, J. (eds) *Research and Practice in Primary Classrooms*, London, Routledge and Kegan Paul.

CFL VISION (1986) *Practical Thinking, Technology Starts Here*, and *Technology Videos for Schools: Primary Compilation*, Wetherby, CFL Vision.

DEPARTMENT OF EDUCATION AND SCIENCE (1978) *Primary Education in England*, London, HMSO.

DEPARTMENT OF EDUCATION AND SCIENCE (1982) *Education 5–9*, London, HMSO.

DEPARTAMENT OF EDUCATION AND SCIENCE (1983) *9–13 Middle Schools*, London, HMSO.

DEPARTMENT OF EDUCATION AND SCIENCE (1985a) *Better Schools*, London, HMSO.

DEPARTMENT OF EDUCATION AND SCIENCE (1985b) *The curriculum from 5–16*, London, HMSO.

DEPARTMENT OF EDUCATION AND SCIENCE (1985c) *Education 8–12 in Combined and Middle Schools*, London, HMSO.

DEPARTMENT OF EDUCATION AND SCIENCE (1987a) *Craft, design and technology from 5–16*, London, HMSO.

DEPARTMENT OF EDUCATION AND SCIENCE (1987b) *The National Curriculum 5–16: a consultation document*, London, HMSO.

DEPARTMENT OF EDUCATION AND SCIENCE (1988a) *Science for ages 5 to 16*, London, DES.

DEPARTMENT OF EDUCATION AND SCIENCE (1988b) *National Curriculum Design and Technology Working Group Interim Report*, London, DES.

DEPARTMENT OF TRADE AND INDUSTRY (1987) *A Case of Primary School Technology* (videotape), London, DTI.

DESIGN COUNCIL (1987a) *Design and Primary Education*, London, Design Council.

DESIGN COUNCIL (1987b) *The Big Paper*, London, Design Council.

EM AND YFA (East Midlands and Yorkshire Forum of Advisers in CDT) (1985) *Designing and Making: Learning Through Craft, Design, Technology*, Wetherby, EM and YFA.

EVANS, P. (undated) *A Case of Primary School Technology*, Nottingham, National Centre for School Technology.

GALTON, M., SIMON, B., and CROLL, P. (1980) *Inside the Primary Classroom*, London, Routledge and Kegan Paul.

HIGHFIELD, P. (1987) Report presented to DES Course N110 Craft Design Technology, University of Loughborough, July 1987.

JINKS, D. (1984) 'Primary Problems', in *School Technology*, September 1984, Nottingham, National Centre for School Technology.

KENT TV (1986) *Primary Technology: A Problem Solving Approach*, and *The Place of Primary Science and Technology*, Sevenoaks, Kent TV.

SCHOOLS COUNCIL (1974) *Art and Craft Education 8–13*, London, Van Nostrand Reinhold.

SELLWOOD, P. (1987) Problem Solving 5–13 Project, London, Department of Trade and Industry.

SHALLCROSS, P. (1983) *Starting Technology*, Leeds, E. J. Arnold.

SHAW, D. M. (1983) *An Introduction to CDT in the Primary School*, Coventry Local Education Authority.

TIMES EDUCATIONAL SUPPLEMENT (1988) 'Timetable for Implementing National Assessment and Testing', 7 October 1988, 4.

WILLIAMS, P. H. M. (1982) *Teaching Craft Design and Technology 5–13*, London, Croom Helm.

WILLIAMS, P. and JINKS, D. (1985) *Design and Technology 5–12*, Lewes, Falmer Press.

Chapter 3

Perspectives on Design and Technology

Les Tickle

In the mid-1970s few teachers had heard of 'craft, design and technology'. CDT as a label for the amalgam of different aspects of the secondary schools' 'practical' curriculum was just emerging. The kinds of knowledge involved in each of the component 'areas' of craft, design, and technology, were being re-evaluated in the process of curriculum change at secondary level. The relationship between these aspects of learning was debated. Their relationship to other parts of the curriculum, their status, and their relevance to changing economic needs began to be considered among people who are powerful in making the school curriculum what it is – teachers, advisers, inspectors, academics, industrialists, examiners, and politicians.

Developments at secondary level were enhanced by major funded curriculum projects in craft and design education and in technology. These in turn had an influence on the work of the Assessment of Performance Unit which had been established in 1974 to monitor standards in schools. It was a matter of a relatively short time before these and other developments affected debate about the primary school curriculum. There the pressure for science increased after the HMI Primary Survey. That coincided with the broader national debates about introducing pupils to computers, about curriculum 'relevance', and about educating a workforce equipped for a twenty-first-century economy and society. Within that context the emergence of CDT appropriate for the primary school curriculum began. It will continue into the 1990s amid the tensions and conflicts which surround a changing curriculum.

Those tensions and conflicts have been described as being, in part, between the *academic*, *utilitarian*, and *pedagogical* traditions of the school curriculum (Goodson, 1983). The nature of particular 'subjects' or areas of the curriculum, the status of subjects, and the relationship between different subjects is bound up in these traditions, and in the tensions within and between them. The academic tradition is that which subscribes to the pursuit of knowledge for the benefits of 'developing the mind'. Utilitarianism tends to see knowledge in terms of its economic and commercial value. It is instrumental towards material ends, rather than the intellectual and spiritual goals of academic study. The pedagogical tradition stems from the aspirations of educators to define the aims of education and to find the best means of transmitting knowledge or fostering its acquisition. These different traditions, or views on the purpose and nature of education, are very closely related to Blyth's (1965) analysis of the primary school traditions — the academic, the elementary, and the child-centred or progressive. From the tussles between different beliefs which people hold about the nature of education, the curriculum and subjects within it are built.

Goodson (1983, 1988) helps us to understand how, in the evolution of school curricula, subjects may grow out of utilitarian origins to become high-status academic subjects. In doing so, he argues, a subject needs to continue to be accepted as vocational, and also needs to appeal to educators and educational policy-makers for its 'appropriate' teaching methods. These tensions occur in a subject's relationship to other subjects. They also affect the way the subject itself comes to be defined internally, as different views about what it should include and how it should be taught seek to prevail.

We are now witnessing some of these stresses, as CDT's proponents seek to establish its place and status in the curriculum, and particularly in primary schools. It is also possible to detect the internal stresses as different interpretations of what the subject should involve are debated: its aims, content, and teaching/learning processes. For example, the craftwork tradition is having to coexist with the designing through problem-solving approach. Both have to respond to the science base of technology. We will see later how in the GCSE examinations these have been resolved by presenting different syllabi. We do not yet know what the resolutions will result in for primary school practice, but it is worth considering some of the background so far.

Although CDT may be regarded as a new area of the primary school curriculum, relevant to the industrial and economic needs of the late twentieth century, its foundations in the education system are not recent. Educators such as Rousseau, Pestalozzi and Froebel proposed the use of activities which would fit within the bounds of CDT as it is now being redefined (Dodd, 1978). However, the association of its activities with vocationalism, and the implications of training for manual labour, meant that in earlier times it was set against academic study, associated mainly with secondary schools, and experienced by boys.

In primary schools the art and craft tradition was linked with the development of manual dexterity and notions of therapy — neither of which carried academic appeal. In practice art and craft remained firmly in the elementary traditions of teaching 'basic skills' by didactic methods. Science barely got a toe-hold in primary schools. What is more, to the extent that creative activities stemmed from the Arts and Crafts Movement of the nineteenth century, they were also associated with attempts to counter technological advances with personal aesthetic creativity. It was left to others, in other parts of the education system, to examine the relationship between industrial developments, aesthetic responses, and pedagogical aims.

The developments of the sloyd-method of teaching crafts in the late nineteenth century was linked directly to industrial needs. It distinguished craft activities from academic study. But it tried to overcome the use of craft exercises solely for developing manual dexterity. Instead it sought teaching methods which would involve students in planning, carrying out, and 'summing up' (evaluating) useful artefacts through a problem-solving process. This was a forerunner to recent proposals, which I will discuss later. However, it did not catch on. Evidence from the first half of the twentieth century shows consistent arguments made in favour of replacing rigid instruction in skills by greater emphasis on intellectual activity and the use of inventiveness in problem-solving (Dodd, 1978). These same arguments are repeated in *Better Schools* (DES, 1985a).

A recorded attempt to resolve the tensions between a broad education, commercially-oriented training, and the provision of a mixture of teaching styles to provide both skills and inventiveness was made by Walter Gropius in setting up the *Bauhaus* in Germany in 1919. He later described the problem and his attempt to solve it:

> As a first step towards the realisation of a much wider plan — in which my primary aim was that the principle of training the individual's natural capacities to grasp life as a whole, a single cosmic entity, should form the basis of instruction throughout the school instead of in only one or two arbitrarily 'specialised' classes — I amalgamated these institutions into a High School for Design.
>
> In carrying out this scheme I tried to solve the ticklish problem of combining imaginative design with technical proficiency. That meant finding a new and hitherto non-existent type of collaborator who could be moulded into being equally proficient in both . . . . The *Bauhaus* workshops were really laboratories for working out practical new designs for present day articles and improving models for mass production. To create type-forms that would meet all technical, aesthetic and commercial demands required a picked staff. It needed a body of men (*sic*) of wide general culture as thoroughly versed in the practical and mechanical sides of design as in its theoretical and formal laws. (Gropius 1936, pages 52–53).

The combination of high-status technical knowledge, utilitarian commercial purposes, and wider cultural and educational aims must have produced more than one ticklish problem. What is most interesting about this account is the attempt to extend the academic and spiritual pursuit of wider cultural aims — the capacity to grasp life as a cosmic entity — to the overtly utilitarian activities of commercial production. In doing so, Gropius had to address the question of pedagogy, and find ways of amalgamating traditional instruction in the crafts with more open methods which allowed for inventiveness. Teaching methods thus included instruction in manual skills as training for hand and eye, and as a first step towards understanding industrial processes. They also went beyond that to provide a range of teaching strategies, including the visual study of design principles, communicating ideas graphically, prototyping, teamwork in developing design ideas and in production, and so on. This attempt to use technical knowledge and proficiency as a means of serving human achievement of excellence in product design, using the advantages of technology while eliminating its drawbacks, represents the core of the curriculum of some design schools in Britain after 1950.

It is the combination of technical knowledge, design processes, manipulative skills, and values and attitudes which have come through to the school curriculum as characteristic of CDT as we now know it. In particular, those qualities were encapsulated in various ways in the major British curriculum development projects for the subject in the 1970s. Project Technology concentrated entirely on the development of the curriculum of older, more able secondary pupils, in the realm of technical control. Electronics, mechanisms, structures, energy, pneumatics, aeronautics, and other topics in the 'high-tech' realm became the mainstay of modules from this project (Schools Council, 1968). The *Design and Craft Education Project*, which aimed to develop the curriculum of lower-achieving secondary pupils, was concerned with extending the materials-based craft curriculum into designing and problem-solving for 'real' contexts (Schools Council, 1974a). The *Art and Craft 8–13 Project* focused on the use of materials for expressive and creative purposes, with intentions to draw upon and link across work in other subjects of the curriculum (Schools Council, 1974b). Critical awareness of environmental and design issues was the focus of *Art and The Built Environment* (Adams and Ward, 1982) developed with older pupils initially, but with a view to its adaptation for primary age groups. *Science 5–13* (Schools Council, 1974c) aimed to develop scientific working procedures and a knowledge of science through the active exploration of environment, materials, and processes. Each in their turn were influential in the practices carried out by some teachers, and the development of an orientation towards problem-solving activities and exploratory learning which has emerged as a feature in recent policy. Yet they had different emphases, and it is worth taking account of those differences when trying to understand the sometimes uneasy alliances which have been struck within CDT as we now see it emerging, especially as it is adapted to the primary age range.

Despite the recent surge of documents and official statements about CDT, it is difficult to grasp a conception of what it is. There is some disagreement about whether it is a subject or not. In 1980 the DES applied the label to the range of learning that goes on in school workshops, and wrote of 'the family of practical activities which give pupils experience of designing and making' (DES, 1980, p. 3). The report included design-based courses as its primary concern. In these, work concerned with the physical and aesthetic qualities of materials, and the acquisition of skills to shape and use them, is emphasized. Such learning involves the ability to identify problems, to design, communicate and carry out possible solutions, and to evaluate the decisions made in producing a solution. This design process represents the core of the activity and learning centres on the procedural steps of design problem-solving. That had become and remains central to conceptions of CDT, and to appropriate teaching methods for some aspects of it.

In 1983 HMI defined the characteristics of CDT as concerned with the cognitive and manipulative skills inherent in designing and making — the ability to identify, examine and solve problems using tools and materials. These components were identifed as designing and making skills (the problem-solving process); knowledge (of materials, techniques and equipment); and values and attitudes. The problem-solving process was set out like a checklist of teaching objectives; a course in CDT, it was said, should enable pupils of all abilities to develop the skills of problem-solving (see Figure 3.1).

Figure 3.1: HMI's list of problem-solving skills

---

1 tackle an appropriate problem;

2 analyze the nature of that problem to determine the exact requirement;

3 identify and collect appropriate data;

4 apply relevant knowledge to the problem;

5 initiate, develop and then communicate design proposals to others using any appropriate technique;

6 decide upon and detail the most appropriate solution for development;

7 plan the method of production;

8 make the solution to the standard required

9 monitor progress throughout the manufacture until a satisfactory conclusion is reached;

10 evaluate both the efficacy and the overall quality of the design solution, be it a product or a system, and suggest lines for future development, should improvement be desired;

11 record the development of the project.

Source: DES, 1983, p. 3.

HMI's use of the word *skills* for the problem-solving process need not be confused with the use of the term as it relates to manipulative, hand-eye coordination. Those sorts of skills are included by HMI within their realm of *knowledge*. The range of knowledge content needed to effect design capabilities is set out by HMI within the categories of aesthetic sensitivity, technology, graphic skills, craft skills, and health and safety awareness. In addition, a cultural and historical perspective of CDT should also be fostered, they claim. In each there is a list of identified skills and abilities in which courses in *secondary* CDT would be expected to equip pupils. I will discuss later how this range of knowledge has come to be adapted for primary education.

In 1982 the DES had featured one member of the 'family' of activities in a special portrait of technology in secondary schools. Its features consisted of a range of categories, or broad groups, which were seen as distinctively 'technological'. The groups included modular courses in technology, within which self-contained units of specific content were studied, such as Structures, Mechanisms, Electronics, Pneumatics, and Energy. A distinctive modular course, Control Technology, was described, in which control concepts and control devices formed the core of study. These in particular included work on electronics, electricity, and mechanics, sometimes linked with computers. Self-contained courses in electronics, in which electronic devices were constructed and used to solve 'problems', such as lighting systems, alarms, or sound-monitoring, were also identified in schools. Together these sorts of units formed the core of school technology which stemmed from Project Technology and associated work. Applied science and engineering, which included mechanical and automotive engineering, as well as materials technology, was another area of activity which had by then developed in schools. These 'practical' studies were supplemented by courses in technological awareness, including the development of pupils' awareness of technological change, and the social implications of it (DES, 1982).

These ranges of knowledge, skills, processes and attitudes have been incorporated into the new conventions which have become GCSE courses. In these, the core elements of CDT — designing and communicating, making, testing, and evaluating — are followed by selected options in which particular areas of content vary. They are identified in the titles of courses:

> **CDT: Design and Communication** (The development of graphic techniques)
> **CDT: Design and Realisation** (Using materials for product design, based on a product 'brief')
> **CDT: Technology** (Achieving control through understanding technology)

These areas combined are said to contain features which noticeably make CDT distinct from other areas of the curriculum — most obviously its practicality, and its requirement to find solutions to real problems (SEC, 1986). This purported distinctness and separateness, the label CDT, and the view that it is a 'subject', are, however, circumvented by the Assessment of Performance Unit. Theirs is an explicit recognition of the confusions which have grown up:

> Because of the cross-curricular nature of design and technological activity, and its relatively recent appearance in schools' curricula there is less clarity and consensus [than in maths and science] about traditions and practices. (APU, 1987, p. 7).

CDT, Technology, Home Economics and Textiles, and Art and Design are seen as having built up coherent but different approaches to design and technological capability and understanding in pupils.

> From a basis of existing practice it is difficult to achieve an acceptable and all embracing definition first of design — and second of technology — and hence 'design and technology'. An appeal to existing examination titles and syllabuses as a source of clarification is also largely unhelpful, as collectively they reflect the confusions that exist. The task of describing the activity must, therefore, involve unravelling the concept of design and technology and identifying contributing elements. (*ibid.*)

In the DES reports of 1980 and 1982 work from the middle years (8 to 13) was seen to involve a shift from the use of practical work for 'expressive' purposes, towards 'functional problem-solving'. In some cases such work included setting simple mechanical problems for pupils to solve, from which they produced working devices or machines. In others it involved testing the properties of materials. Occasionally work in schools was reportedly being done on tasks such as making electrical circuits, which required the learning of specific technological concepts. However, nowhere did HMI report a coherent policy or strategy for the conduct of CDT in primary schools. Nor did they report on work with children younger than 8.

The first collected evidence of such work was included in the *Designing and Making* Exhibition (EM and YFA, 1985). The coordinators were cautious about using the label CDT in relation to primary schools. Rather, they offered a broad definition of the subject and gave some indication of what it involves as an activity:

> Craft, Design, Technology, is the name of a subject found in the curriculum of secondary schools which has as its particular focus the man-made world of objects and devices. The subject title is unlikely to be used in primary schools although its focus, and the kinds of work that characterise it as an activity, are certainly to be found there. Designing and making is a more generic application than Craft, Design, Technology, and for that reason is used as the main title for the exhibition and for this booklet. (EM and YFA, 1985, p. 3).

The essence of this generic activity, they demonstrated, begins at a very early age, in the development of sensory-motor and intellectual capability through the handling of materials. The manipulation, control and use of materials, knowledge of their properties, and concepts of function, for example, are seen as central to CDT and to early childhood exploration in learning. What is more, the capacity of young children to engage in the essential elements of the design process is summed up from observations of children working with materials:

> a process of designing and making is in operation in which there is a constant inter-action between the elements of discovery, thinking, investigating, decision-making, problem-solving, constructing, evaluating and modification. (EM and YFA, 1985, p. 6).

The Design Council, too, found problems in defining design and design education, recognizing the various links with art, crafts, technology, and science. The common element of what it chose to call 'design-related activities' was set out clearly as a process:

> Design is the way in which we try to shape our environment, both in its whole and in its parts. Anybody setting out to design anything — an object, a room, a garden, a process or an event — will be trying to mould the materials, space, time, and other resources which are available to meet a need which she or he has identified. (Design Council, 1987, para. 3.3).

It is not difficult to relate such a concept to the spontaneous activities of play in which young children engage. When the process is abstracted and formalized, however, it seems to be distanced from the realities of practical activities through which children learn. Seeing the process in terms of identifying a problem, assembling information, deciding upon and producing a solution, and evaluating and modifying it, may put a strait-jacket on thinking about such activities for primary school teachers. For younger children in particular the practice of such design activities is not so clear-cut or sequential.

Also, there is a general and widespread tension for teachers engaged in the education of young children. It is that the qualities which are said to be 'required' for the successful conduct of designing (i.e. the application of this design process) are slowly being *acquired*. An understanding of spatial relationships, visual awareness, and the capability to use and understand materials, for example, are qualities *to be developed* (Design Council, 1987, para. 3.5). So is the ability to make aesthetic judgements, to appreciate environmental issues, or to understand mechanical or structural concepts. The tension is that in the jigsaw of skills, knowledge, values and attitudes which make up these capabilities, children may not always be in a position to demonstrate their achievements. This is a puzzle which will only be solved slowly, each teacher with each child fitting the pieces as the connections are spotted. There is no prescribed or ready-made syllabus. It will be necessary for teachers to select which aspects of the skills, knowledge, values and attitudes to seek to develop at specific stages in pupils' experience.

Such choices will not be easy, because of the differences in the nature of knowledge and curriculum objectives which have emerged within the CDT label. For example the question of the relationship between 'expressive' purposes and 'functional problem-solving' was raised again by HMI in *The Curriculum from 5–16* (DES, 1985b). The areas of experience outlined in that document as the basis for the curriculum of all schools include the aesthetic and creative, the scientific, and the technological. These areas of experience have equivalents related directly to the primary school curriculum in the white paper *Better Schools*. Craft, design and technology is mentioned in addition to the arts, science and technology with an explicit intention that these should not be regarded as discrete areas, nor taught separately and in isolation from each other (DES, 1985a, pp. 16–20). Yet the emphasis in the aesthetic and creative area is clearly concerned with emotions and feelings, as well as intellect and inventing. It is affective, personal responses to seen, heard, and felt experiences which underlie the need to acquire knowledge and skills which would enable expression in suitable media — music, dance, drama, and visual art.

The realm of science, on the other hand, is concerned with pupils' knowledge and understanding of the natural and man-made world, and with the procedures of scientific investigation. An emphasis on these empirical procedures, of observation, conducting tests, recording, analyzing, and interpreting, distinguishes this area from the aesthetic aspects of the curriculum. Its base is the rational and logical consideration of problems. In the expressive arts, the assumptions of rationality and logic do not necessarily prevail. In *Better Schools* a conception of the *technological* area of the curriculum is presented as overtly utilitarian, as the activity which enables efficient and effective work to be conducted, for the sake of more, better and cheaper products. The commercial connotations are accompanied by notions of the advancement of human achievements, but they are distinctly not in the realm of personal expression. The essence of technology lies in the knowledge required to implement effectively the process of problem-solving as a means of effecting control. That includes control over materials, through understanding their properties and potential for use. It also involves understanding features of our environment such as the sources and functions of energy, the nature and principles of structures and forces which affect them, and the principles by which mechanisms operate to enable machines to be constructed and to function efficiently. Increasingly, too, knowledge of information technology, especially the handling of computers as tools of control over the functions of machines, is part of that essential knowledge base.

These broad conceptions of CDT have more recently been summarized in a statement of its purpose as seen by HMI. It is, they say:

to enable pupils to be inventive in designing practical solutions to problems and so bring about change and improvements in existing situations. In CDT ideas are conceived, developed, modified and given shape in artefacts through which the original ideas can be evaluated.' (DES, 1987a, para. 1).

That purpose is elaborated into a set of aims for the subject which, it is asserted, should be achieved during the period of compulsory schooling. These include the ability to communicate in practical contexts, presumably orally and in written and graphic forms. The development of confidence and competence to identify, examine and solve practical problems reasserts the essence of CDT already discussed in so many sources. The development of pupils' understanding of the ways in which products or systems might be controlled and how they might be made to work more effectively brings control technology fully within the precincts of CDT, with function as a central concept. Critical and appreciative aspects of learning are included through the aim to encourage pupils to make judgments of the aesthetic, economic, social and technological quality of their own work and that of others (DES, 1987a, para. 7).

The detailed objectives for CDT set out by HMI for pupils up to the age of 11 indicate more specifically the kinds of activities in which they believe pupils ought to be engaged in primary schools. These, with some modification and addition, can be profiled as shown in Figure 3.2. What had become the characteristic content and working procedures of CDT at secondary school level were here represented in a simpler form, their foundations to be laid throughout the primary school curriculum.

The progress of craft, design and technology has been rapid since the unexpected inclusion of technology as one of the nine curriculum areas in *The curriculum from 5–16* (DES, 1985b), followed by its inclusion in the Education Reform Act as one of the foundation subjects of the national curriculum. It is the only foundation subject accorded the same priority as the core subjects of English, mathematics, and science, in its immediate referral to a subject working group of the National Curriculum Council. The result is a set of proposals for introduction in the early stages of implementation of the national curriculum. The definitions of, and perspectives on, CDT for 5-to-11-year-olds have taken an interesting course in this short period.

The National Curriculum Council science working group also considered *Technology 5–11*. The content and working procedures of CDT set out by HMI appear to have been incorporated into the group's recommendations. It defined technology as being concerned with problem-solving through designing and making artefacts to meet a purpose. Such activity, it reasserts, involves the need to investigate, innovate, make and evaluate, drawing upon a wide range of knowledge and skills, especially from craft and design, economics, mathematics, and science (DES, 1988a, paras 5.1–5.12). Here the proposals ran into the problems of defining curriculum according to subjects, for the knowledge, skills, attitudes and understanding which are labelled within each of these 'contributory' areas were certainly not confined to them.

From craft and design, it was said, pupils would be expected to encounter materials and learn the ways they can be worked; to know tools and safe methods for their use; to understand aesthetic factors (including effects of colour, pattern and texture); and to develop the ability to communicate design ideas. Economics would be incorporated through consideration of the availability and cost of materials, the processes used and the time taken in production. Mathematical knowledge, skill and understanding would include those of shapes (two- and

Figure 3.2: HMI objectives for CDT up to age 11

CRAFT

know the qualities of different materials;

know the names and purposes of tools and equipment;

use effectively and safely a variety of tools to fashion materials;

cut, join and rearrange pliable materials;

DESIGN

seek and record information from sources;

analyze and synthesize ideas and formulate a plan of action;

communicate ideas about ways of carrying out a task;

make prototype models;

make working models;

appreciate aesthetic properties of finished materials;

EVALUATION

explain the work they are doing, and give and receive advice;

judge the merits of solutions to a problem;

recognize how a product may be improved;

TECHNOLOGY

know the characteristic properties of common materials;

understand sources of energy;

be familiar with ways of using energy;

know the rates and measurement of energy transfer;

understand the generation of movement;

understand structural qualities;

understand the working principles of mechanisms;

appreciate the combination of energy, materials, and mechanisms to produce artefacts.

Source: DES, 1987a, para. 7.

three-dimensional); spatial awareness; the ability to use scale; and the ability to estimate, compute and measure. Scientific skills of exploration and investigation were included, together with knowledge of materials and their properties. Understanding of forces and structures, and energy and the way it is controlled, were also drawn from the domain of science in the group's recommendations.

Thus the content was initially defined in broad terms, just as the procedure for designing and making was set out by the working group as a simple 'design line', by way of which pupils would be expected to show evidence of:

Observation,
investigation
and enquiry
    Recording
      Designing
        Making
          Evaluating.

The more detailed proposals for the programme of study, attainment targets and assessment in technology in the national curriculum need to be understood within the context of the recommendations of the Task Group on Assessment and Testing (TGAT) (DES, 1988c). The proposals of the TGAT have been a basis on which the subject groups' recommendations, and their eventual implementation in the national curriculum, have been made. Within the TGAT proposals a central idea was to identify a range of *profile components* each of which would cover an aspect of learning within a core or foundation subject of the national curriculum. In the case of primary technology the science working group recommended that there should be one profile component — Technology 5 to 11.

In line with the recommendations of the TGAT, the *programme of study* proposed for Technology 5 to 11 was to be subdivided in relation to four *attainment targets*:

1. Technology in context
   Children should know that the response to the needs of the living and man-made world has often resulted in a technological solution. They should understand that there can be benefits and drawbacks, and realise that this has implications for their own lives, that of the community and the way we make decisions.
2. Designing and Making
   Children should be able to design and make an artefact, product or system. They should be able to select and use materials to match specific needs; be able to use tools safely to cut, join and mould them with due regard to aesthetic and functional properties.
3. Using Forces and Energy
   Children should be able to develop and use their knowledge and understanding of forces — both static (in structures) and dynamic (in moving things). They should develop and use their knowledge and understanding of energy, its sources, uses and ways of controlling it.
4. Communicating Technology
   Children should be able to communicate clearly their stages of thinking, designing and making and evaluating using a variety of means such as modelling, drawing,

oral or written, mathematical or computer techniques. They should be able to select the most appropriate method for the audience or purpose. (DES, 1988a, pp. 76–82).

For each of the primary technology attainment targets a relevant part of the programme of study was prescribed for children in each of the TGAT's proposed *key stages* of 5 to 7 and 7 to 11 years. The science group's programme is set out in Appendix 1.

The TGAT report pointed out that the educational purpose of the national curriculum is to work for the achievement of the attainment targets within each subject for all pupils. For them to achieve maximum personal levels requires that assessment of achievement should be criterion-referenced, with criteria defined in terms of *levels of achievement*. The report proposed that there should be ten levels for the 5 to 16 age range. Each level might be achieved by different pupils at different ages. The levels of achievement were, and are, intended as sequences or stages of progression, such that a pupil might be expected to progress through each level in turn. Detailed criteria for each level of achievement, in relation to each attainment target in Technology 5 to 11 proposed in the national curriculum subject working group report *Science for ages 5 to 16* (DES, 1988a) are also included in Appendix 1. The criteria were set out as *statements of attainment* for each level of achievement. It was, and is, the intention of the TGAT that assessments of the achievements of individual pupils should be made, recorded, and reported to parents towards the end of each of the *key stages*. This would be done as an 'aggregated' score for the single profile component in the case of primary technology. (The TGAT also intended that scores by groups of pupils might be further aggregated to indicate overall standards in a school, local education authority, and the country as a whole).

The science working group report was published in August 1988 in 'consultation' form. A month earlier the NCC design and technology working group, which had initially been established to consider only the secondary phase (key stages 3 and 4), had *its* remit extended to include primary technology. Its interim report, published in November 1988, was clear that the science group's work had been 'useful' but that it had not been directly drawn upon in formulating attainment targets and programmes of study (DES, 1988b, para. 2.3). What the design and technology group reported at that stage can perhaps best be understood from its discussion of 'definition and scope':

> A point of definition that requires immediate comment concerns the use of the dual term design and technology. Our understanding is that whereas most, but not all, design activities will generally include technology and most technology activities will include design, there is not always total correspondence.
>
> Our use of design and technology as a unitary concept, to be spoken in one breath as it were, does not therefore embody redundancy. It is intended to emphasise the intimate connection between the two activities as well as to imply a concept which is broader than either design or technology individually and the whole of which we believe is educationally important.
>
> It may be objected that such usage devalues craft and that the most appropriate title would be craft, design and technology, one which is already widely adopted, at least in secondary schools. There is certainly no intention to imply that craft skills are unimportant; they are essential means to the achievement of many design goals; indeed, paragraph 6 of our terms of reference states explicitly that pupils should be taught 'the practical craft skills needed for realising their designs'. (DES, 1988b, paras 1.5–1.7).

23

The final report of the working group confirmed that aspects of craftmanship should be developed at every stage of design and technology activity (DES, 1989, para. 1.18). The report followed immediately, though briefly, with the use of CDT as a substituted 'unitary concept'. In its further deliberations it was clear that design and technology was seen as distinctive, particularly from science, because of its practical, purposeful nature and cognitive processes of imaging, formulating, and realizing problems and solutions in social and environmental contexts. Critical reflection upon and appraisal of solutions is a further distinctive quality of design and technology posited by the group as rationale for its place in the national curriculum (DES, 1988b, paras 1.11 and 1.12).

The recommendations for attainment targets and programmes of study, it was emphasized, were provisional and speculative. The group acknowledged that it was required to address complex matters about which there is little or no research, nor any school curriculum tradition from which to draw the experience of professional practice. Thus the report stated:

> Indeed one interpretation of our task is that of contributing to the establishment of a traditon in the new curriculum area. (*ibid.*, para. 1.15).

That contribution began with a modest yet fundamental consideration of the nature of the knowledge involved in designing and making. The group considered the eclectic use of knowledge by designers who draw from any useful discipline or source, with an 'unbounded' view of knowledge, unrestrained by classifications or 'subjects'. It also considered the ways in which school knowledge is often classified and constrained by narrow labels, even within specific school subjects. While the group sympathized with the eclectic use of knowledge, it rejected 'complete openness' on the pragmatic ground that it would be too daunting for teachers to operate in schools. However it rejected as unsatisfactory the tight parcelling of knowledge, arguing that it would be incompatible with the nature of design and technological activities set in a broad range of social and environmental contexts. In doing so it was implicitly critical of developments in GCSE courses, and of aspects of the science group's recommendations for primary technology.

The combination of professional pragmatism and epistemological openness resulted in recommendations by the design and technology group of a 'process perspective'. In this perspective designing activity is paramount, but supported by a base of knowledge and skills 'prescribed in sufficient detail to give some structure in support of the planning by teachers of design and technology activities' (*ibid.*, para. 1.26). It was acknowledged that one of the central cognitive elements of designing and making is the formulation and application of a wide range of *judgments*. The notion of educational progression was seen as partly concerned with increasing the sophistication of 'the art of making these judgements which are characteristic of the world of practical action' (*ibid.*, para. 1.32). (Progression is also seen in part as accumulation of knowledge and skills which resource the making of judgments, and as a broadening of contexts and constrains which apply to the activity of designing). This conception of the design process as a holistic activity leading to artefacts or systems, and critical appraisal of them, established the group's direction of thinking away from 'knowledge-led attainment targets', within the single profile component of *Design and Technological Capability*. The final report's four attainment targets, which differ markedly from the four proposed by the science group, were regarded as integral to and always all involved in the activity of design and technology. They are in essence the characteristic 'design line', 'design loop', 'design cycle' or 'design interaction' devised and refined by proponents of craft, design and technology. Giving these elements the status of attainment targets clearly established the design process as the intended central feature of the experiences of pupils, in the development of design and technological capability (see Figure 3.3).

Figure 3.3: Attainment targets

Profile Component: Design and Technological capability

AT1 **Identifying needs and opportunities**	AT2 **Generating a design proposal**	AT3 **Planning and making**	AT4 **Appraising**
Through exploration and investigation of a range of contexts (home; school; recreation, community; business and industry) pupils should be able to identify and state clearly needs and opportunities for design and technological activites.	Pupils should be able to produce a realistic, appropriate and achievable design by generating, exploring and developing design and technological ideas and by refining and detailing the design and proposal they have chosen.	Working to a plan derived from their previously developed design, pupils should be able to identify, manage and use appropriate resources, including both knowledge and processes, in order to make an artefact, system or environment.	Pupils should be able to develop, communicate and act constructively upon an appraisal of the processes, outcomes and effects of their own design and technological activity as well as of the outcomes and effects of design and technological activity of others, including those from other times and cultures.

Source: DES, 1989

In recognition of the need to specify and prescribe a range of knowledge and understanding upon which to structure curriculum planning in schools, the interim report proposed four domains of knowledge which it regarded as constituting a core resource for activities, to be acquired by age 16 + . These are summarized in Figure 3.4. The categories are incorporated into the *programmes of study* of the final report (see Appendix 2).

Figure 3.4: Design and Technology Knowledge Resource Base

---

1. Media for Design and Technology Activities:
materials and components
energy
information

2. Influences on Design and Technology Practice:
business and economics
tools and equipment
mathematics
aesthetics

3. Characteristics of Design and Technology Products:
aesthetics
systems
structures
mechanisms

4. Applications and Effects of Design and Technology Activities:
economic
social
technological

Source: DES, 1988b, para. 2.25.

A major part of the task of the design and technology working group (in common with all the other NCC subject groups) was to amplify the attainment targets and programmes of study into detailed statements of attainment, linked to ten levels of achievement specified by the TGAT. Unlike the presentation by the science working group, the design and technology interim report acknowledged that this was extremely difficult because of the lack of understanding about assessment and pupil achievement in design and technology. The group's objection to knowledge-led and/or skills-led attainment targets, and the centrality of performance in design and technological capability, made their task a considerable challenge:

> the highly integrative nature of design and technology makes it impossible to tease out, and isolate for assessment purposes, discrete sub-processes of the holistic activity. Instead, we attempt in the attainment targets to identify educationally valid learning outcomes from the design and technological activity which can be assessed, and reported on, as worthwhile in their own right. Furthermore, we argue that it is reasonable, within the TGAT framework, to aggregate performances on these five[1] tasks into a score for our proposed profile component of design and technological capability. (*ibid.*, para. 2.16).

Likewise the interim report provided an accompanying list of skills which were seen as complementary to the functional core of knowledge and understanding. In doing so it was acknowledged that this meant 'engaging in the task of dividing the indivisible' in order to be in keeping with prevailing curriculum terminology, and for ease of reference. Different ways of setting out the skills-resource base were considered, and an arrangement chosen which presented 'clusters which have some internal coherence' rather than a definitive list. The clusters were identified only as broad headings to indicate the range of skills consistent with the attainment targets (see Figure 3.5).

Figure 3.5: Design and Technology Skills Resource Base

1. exploring and investigating

2. imaging and speculating

3. organizing and planning

4. making

5. communicating and presenting

6. appraising

Source: DES, 1988b, para. 2.32.

The complexity of the work needed to address these questions, leading to statements of attainment and programmes of study linked to levels of achievement, formulated on the basis of 'professional judgements', is reflected in the final report of the Design aand Technology Working Group (DES, 1989). Details are set out in Appendix 2 for key stages 1 and 2 (5–7 years and 7–11 years).

Note

1 The interim report proposed five attainment targets, which were reduced to four in the final report.

References

ADAMS, E., and WARD, C. (1982) *Art and the Built Environment*, London, Longman.
ASSESSMENT OF PERFORMANCE UNIT (1987) *Design and Technological Activity: a framework for assessment*, London, HMSO.
BLYTH, W.A.L. (1965) *English Primary Education: A Sociological Description*, London, Routledge and Kegan Paul.
BRUNER, J. (1960) *The Process of Education*, Cambridge, Mass., Harvard University Press.
DEPARTMENT OF EDUCATION AND SCIENCE (1980) *Craft, Design and Technology in Schools: some successful examples*, London, HMSO.
DEPARTMENT OF EDUCATION AND SCIENCE (1982) *Technology in Schools*, London, HMSO.

DEPARTMENT OF EDUCATION AND SCIENCE (1983) *CDT: A curriculum statement for the 11–16 + age group*, London, DES.

DEPARTMENT OF EDUCATION AND SCIENCE (1985a) *Better Schools*, London, HMSO.

DEPARTMENT OF EDUCATION AND SCIENCE (1985b) *The curriculum from 5–16*, London, HMSO.

DEPARTMENT OF EDUCATION AND SCIENCE (1987a) *Craft, design and technology from 5–16*, London, HMSO.

DEPARTMENT OF EDUCATION AND SCIENCE (1987b) *The National Curriculum: a consultation document*, London, HMSO.

DEPARTMENT OF EDUCATION AND SCIENCE (1988a) *Science for ages 5 to 16*, London, DES.

DEPARTMENT OF EDUCATION AND SCIENCE (1988b) *National Curriculum Design and Technology Working Group Interim Report*, London, DES.

DEPARTMENT OF EDUCATION AND SCIENCE (1988c) *Task Group on Assessment and Testing: A Report*, London, DES.

DEPARTMENT OF EDUCATION AND SCIENCE (1989) *National Curriculum Design and Technology Working Group Report*, London, DES.

DESIGN COUNCIL (1987) *Design and Primary Education*, London, Design Council.

DODD, T. (1978) *Design and Technology in the School Curriculum*, London, Hodder and Stoughton.

EM and YFA (EAST MIDLANDS AND YORKSHIRE FORUM OF ADVISERS CDT) (1985) *Designing and Making: Learning through craft, design, technology*, Wetherby, EM and YFA.

GOODSON, I.F. (1983) *School Subjects and Curriculum Change*, London, Croom Helm.

GOODSON, I.F. (1988) *The Making of Curriculum*, Lewes, Falmer Press.

GROPIUS, W. (1936) *The New Architecture and The Bauhaus*, London, Faber (1965 edition).

SCHOOLS COUNCIL (1968) *Project Technology*, Nottingham, National Centre for Schools Technology.

SCHOOLS COUNCIL (1974a) *Design and Craft Education Project*, Leeds, Edward Arnold.

SCHOOLS COUNCIL (1974b) *Art and Craft Education 8–13*, London, Van Nostrand Reinhold.

SCHOOLS COUNCIL (1974c) *Science 5–13*, London, Macdonald.

SECONDARY EXAMINATIONS COUNCIL (1986) *GCSE Craft, Design and Technology*, Milton Keynes, Open University Press.

Chapter 4

Developing Practical Knowledge for Teaching Design and Technology

Les Tickle, Mike Lancaster, Mark Devereux and Eric Marshall

At the stages of both initial and in-service teacher education fostering the complex range of knowledge needed for primary teaching is a difficult process, because there are so many elements which have to be learnt, blended together, and put into action for teaching in an orchestrated way. In the content of the curriculum (whether it is separated into subjects or dealt with in an integrated way) the vast range of skills, knowledge and understanding which has to be dealt with by teachers is often daunting. In the case of 'new' areas of the curriculum like CDT acquisition of knowledge and implementation of classroom practice can be even more difficult than in other areas because there is no tradition or foundation laid during school or higher education for most teachers. It will be several generations before we have a teaching force whose members all experienced CDT, or technology, or science, as part of their own education. As a consequence it is not uncommon to hear the fears and anxieties of student–teachers and teachers who are not familiar with the territory of CDT being expressed loudly and clearly. At times one might think some teachers would rather handle a deadly cobra!

Yet if new learning opportunities are regarded constructively, a lack of expertise can be translated into a new, potential acquisition. Or, more realistically, a set of acquisitions which can be built up over a period of time, introduced into the repertoire of practical teaching knowledge gradually.

The previous chapters have shown from evidence of existing practice the need to develop designing and making and technological activities in the primary school curriculum. That development will depend very heavily upon the identification, acquisition and further improvement of the practical knowledge of CDT: the skills, knowledge, attitudes and beliefs of the teachers who would be instrumental in introducing the activities of designing and making to pupils. I will show in this chapter how practical knowledge of CDT content and teaching strategies can grow through an accretion of experience by taking some examples as starting points. However, the practical knowledge of teaching is more than just subject matter. Elbaz (1983) has shown the importance of the relationship between, for example, knowing: *oneself* as a teacher; the working circumstances and '*milieu*' of the school; the particular *pupils*; the *subject matter*; *teaching methods* related to it; and *evaluation techniques* for ensuring effective teaching. It is within that range of practical knowledge, the combination of which makes teaching individualized and unique to each teacher, that this chapter takes the risk of separating out some elements of subject matter and teaching strategies.

In CDT 'subject matter' does not refer solely to knowledge content, as the earlier sections of this book show. Thus experience and understanding of the designing process needs to be acquired. Engaging in 'open-ended' activities may be threatening to some teachers, products themselves of an education system which gives credits for fixed knowledge, correct answers and set quantities of recitation. First and foremost in such cases it is necessary to experience problem-solving in order to understand the nature of CDT and the principles of some of its teaching strategies.

In our own realm of expertise, teaching, we engage in problem-solving a great deal. It is so taken for granted as part of the job that it is often not considered as a design process. The classroom is a system which the teacher has partly designed. Within the fixed constraints of architecture, resources, numbers of pupils and their characteristics, the design results from having analyzed the problem, taken account of evidence, implemented a plan of action, and evaluated and modified the outcome. What is different in the case of CDT is the nature of the problem, the materials available, and the knowledge brought to bear upon them.

Like the task of teaching, the design process cannot be standardized to make it administratively tidy. Yet, also like teaching, there are sensible procedures which, with flexibility and willingness to change direction, provide guidance in problem-solving. A further similarity is that it is not sufficient to know *about* problem-solving; it is necessary to know *how*. Being capable in know-how presents a special problem in developing practical knowledge, for it requires time to assimilate information and the experience of practice. It is necessary to work step by step, dealing with digestible amounts. Risks, failures, retrials and successes all have to be accommodated in the accretion of experience, often in situations of uncertainty and decision-making. Illustration 4.1 is from work by Mike Lancaster, showing some of the thinking processes involved in situations where there are no given answers. Nor are there necessarily correct ways of going about the search for solutions to the problem posed. Mike had already developed some skills in graphic communication and in handling materials and tools. A range of knowledge and skills already held needed to be applied to the problem. Further skills had to be acquired during the process of solving it.

A design brief was given: *using wood design and make a toy to help hand-eye co-ordination and manipulative skills in young children. It must be safe, tough and appealing.*

The stages in designing included: investigating the fine motor development of young children; thinking of ideas and matching them to the design brief; sketching several possibilities and considering their feasibility; deciding on a solution and elaborating the design details; discussing the proposal to hear other suggestions and points of view; drafting in detail to communicate the ideas in graphic form, both as a working drawing and as demonstration of the plan. The later parts of the designing stage and the final product are shown in illustration 4.1.

In the example of Mike Lancaster's work, *isometric paper* was introduced, its use demonstrated by the tutor, and used for initial sketches. Graphic techniques were also discussed and possibilities introduced through the use of books of design and communication methods (Beasley, 1984; Light, 1988). A range of media used in graphic design was made available, including technical design boards and suitable pencils, crayons and marker pens. Together with appropriate instruction and expectations these ensured the use and development of skilled drafting.

Illustration 4.1

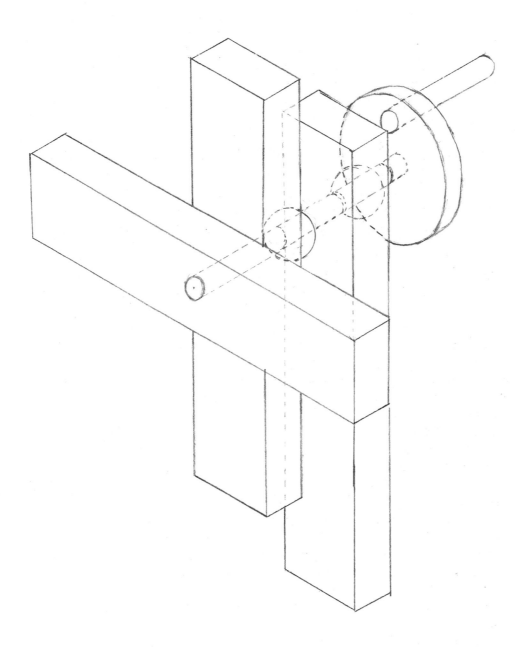

(i) A drawing at the later stage of designing

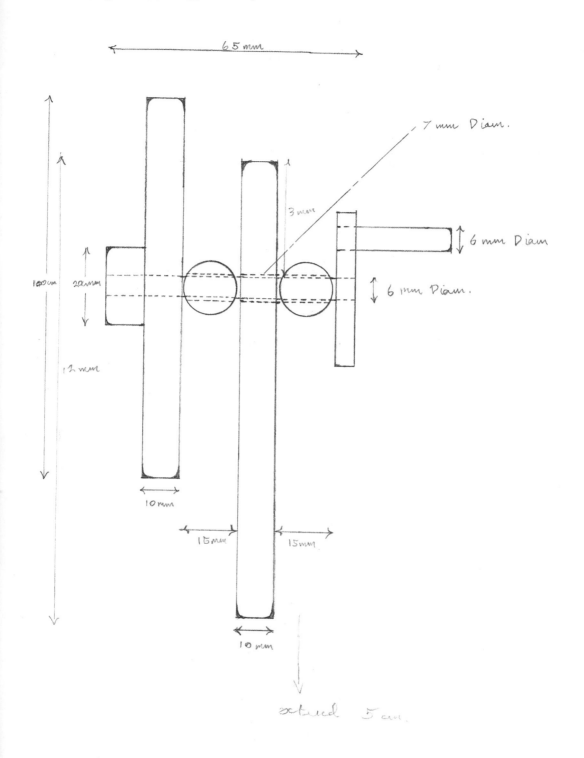

65 mm

7 mm Diam.

3 mm

6 mm Diam

6 mm Diam.

100 cm

20 mm

12 mm

10 mm

15 mm

15 mm

10 mm

actual 5 cm.

(ii) A working drawing

MATERIALS.

1. 320 × 20 × 10mm length of wood

2. 95 mm length 6 mm Diam. dowel.

3. 40 mm Diam. wheel.

4. Two 15mm Diam beads.

All edges to be
rounded of.

Alternative to beads
might be lengths of
plastic tubing.

Painted bright colours
or varnished.

(iii) Some notes to the working drawing

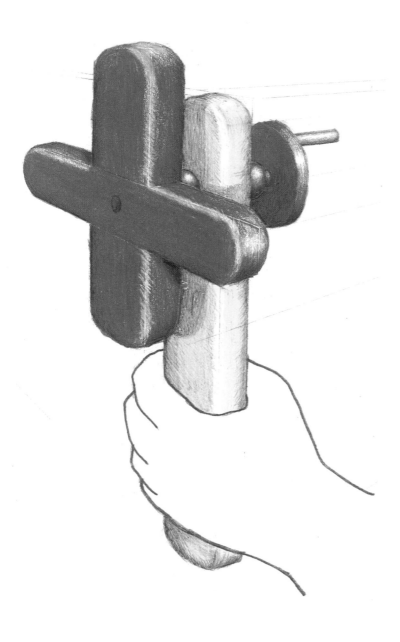

(iv) A final illustration of the design

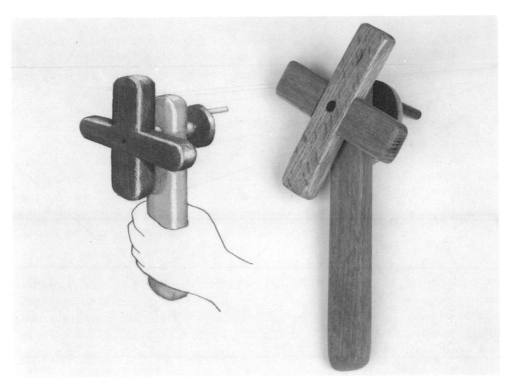

(v) The final product

(vi) A different solution to the same design brief

The detailed knowledge brought to bear upon a problem, and thus the knowledge which teachers need to acquire to be competent in problem-solving (and then in teaching pupils and helping them to be problem-solvers) will come from within a broad set of skills, knowledge and understanding. The further progress of Mike Lancaster's work is used to illustrate those areas of knowledge as they combine with stages in problem-solving. Thus after the graphic stage of designing, the stages in making the toy included choosing suitable materials, measuring and marking the wood, cutting and joining it, and providing suitable finishes to the surface.

Each of these steps required either the application of existing know-how by Mike, discussion, or instruction from the tutor. Knowledge of wood, which is tough, was essential to satisfy the design brief. The accurate use of ruler and tri-square was important to the execution of the design. The use of a bench vice, bench hook, hand-saw, drill, and glue-gun effected the cutting and joining stages. Use of sandpaper, paint and polyurethane completed the visual and tactile qualities of the toy.

The elements of technology involved in this design were not extensive, nor were they consciously incorporated when the idea was conceived. However, during boths stages of the production it is clear that some knowledge of mechanisms and movement was incorporated, together with questions of the control of speed, and implicit was the source and transmission of energy. Through a play item, and in a very simple way, Mike was here including experiences for the users of the toy which would enable later, conscious consideration of such technological concepts.

The evaluation of the ideas, the design, and the function of the toy was a continuous process which illustrates the uncertainties inherent in problem-solving. For instance, during making, the design was modified at various stages, after judgments had been made, to include a lengthened handle; rounded corners to the sails for safety and tactile improvement; the bead washer replaced by a plastic tube, then by a metal washer to make the mechanism more efficient; a shortened shaft to reduce wobble on the sails; the insertion of a plastic 'bush' to secure the shaft; and the use of natural wood-grain surface, with highlighted colour for the mechanism only.

Each of the broad realms of skill, knowledge and understanding, from which Mike was using and learning specific items, has a long and detailed set of subskills and knowledge. It is not my intention to catalogue these here, since details can be found in other sources. Table 4.1 outlines some of the broad areas of knowledge and indicates sources from which more extensive information can be found.

The example of the small toy, combining the problem-solving process with the acquisition and application of skills, knowledge and understanding, serves also to illustrate how such tasks and experiences can be translated into teaching strategies. That needs to be done in ways appropriate to particular contexts, resources and pupils so that design tasks are modified and presented to ensure that specific knowledge and skills are encountered. A series of further examples of design tasks can be found in the sources for developing classroom projects listed in Table 4.1. Other examples and detailed analysis of pupils' responses to problem-solving form the later chapters of this book.

Illustration 4.2 shows work by Mark Devereux based on considerations of wind power and energy, which includes a different range of knowledge and skills from the first example. The materials, tools, and concepts vary from some of those invoked by Mike Lancaster's project, by virtue of the different nature of the task. In this instance the starting point was a topical news item concerning the intention to build test-beds in Britain for harnessing wind power as part of the nation's energy supply.

Illustration 4.2

Some test models

Through modelling Mark set out to make and test different mechanisms for harnessing wind energy, using materials which would be available in the primary school classroom.

Once again the combination of thought processes and knowledge/skills can be seen. The initial sketching of ideas and possibilities, the choice and use of suitable materials and tools to effect some of the ideas, testing of the models, and making modifications to construction techniques and mechanisms, all played a part in the development of the project. The use of judgments and decision-making, and the acquisition of new knowledge, skills, and understanding which resulted, are complex. For example, design and technological considerations included the surface area, shape and weight of sails on the windmills. These were related in testing to questions about harnessing and transmitting the energy for use through other mechanisms. Their construction required consideration of structures and structural properties, incorporating skills which ranged from sticking pointed garden canes firmly and accurately into a bottle cork, to accurate drilling in the edge of a wooden disc.

*Table 4.1: Sources for Developing Knowledge/
Gaining Information*

Areas covered	Graphic Techniques	Craft Skills	Tools/Equipment	Materials	Technology	Health and Safety	Social Context	Classroom Projects
Berkshire LEA, Shire Hall, Reading, Berks., *Primary Craft Design and Technology; A Talent for Technology; Technology.*								•
Breckon, A., and Prest, D., *Introducing Craft Design and Technology*, Hutchinson and Co., 17–21 Conway Street, London W1P 6JD.	•	•	•	•	•	•	•	•
British Gas Education Service, PO Box 46, Hounslow, Middx TW4 6NF.					•	•	•	•
Cement and Concrete Association, Fulmer Grange, Fulmer, Slough, SL2 4QS.		•	•	•	•	•	•	•
Central Electricity Generating Board, 15 Newgate Street, London EC1B 1BY.					•	•	•	•
Davis Publications/Lewis Brooks Ltd, 2 Blagdon Road, New Malden, Surrey KT3 4AD.	•	•	•	•	•	•	•	•
Department of Energy Education Unit, Thames House South, Millbank, London SW1P 4QJ.					•	•	•	•
Education Service of the Plastics Industry, University of Technology, Loughborough, LE11 3TU.		•	•	•	•	•	•	•
Fitchett and Woollacott Ltd, Willow Road, Lenton Lane, Nottingham NG7 2PR.					•			
Health Education Council, 78 New Oxford Street, London WC1A 1AH.						•		
ICI Petrochemicals and Plastics Division, PO Box 6, Bessemer Road, Welwyn Garden City, Herts AL7 1HD.					•	•	•	•
Kent Educational TV Centre, Barton Road, Dover, Kent CT16 2ND.		•	•	•	•	•	•	•

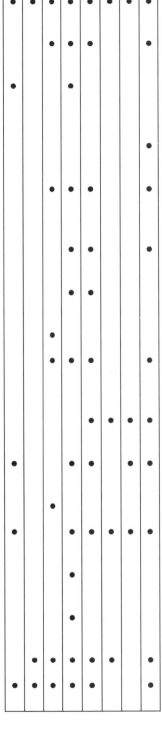

Kimbell, R., *GCSE Craft Design and Technology*, Hutchinson Education, 62–65 Chandos Place, London WC2N 4NW.

Lego UK Limited Education Division, Ruthin Road, Wrexham, Clwyd, LL13 7TQ.

Light, B. *Starting Design and Communication*, Longman Group UK Limited, Longman House, Burnt Mill, Harlow, Essex.

London Borough of Barnet Education Department, *Primary School Craft Design and Technology*.

Mills, G., and Aitken, J., *First Steps in Technology* and *Creative Technology*, Holmes McDougall, Allander House, 137–141 Leith Walk, Edinburgh EH6 8NS.

Peter Huxtable Designs Ltd, *40 CDT Projects*, Merritts, Great Witley, Worcester WR6 6JG.

Rapid Electronics Ltd, Hill Farm Industrial Estate, Boxted, Colchester CO4 5RS.

Record Marples Ltd, Parkway Works, Sheffield.

Shallcross, P., *Starting Technology — The Simple Approach*, E. J. Arnold, Parkside Lane, Dewsbury Road, Leeds LS11 5TD.

Shell Education Service (Shell UK Ltd), Shell-Mex House, Strand, London WC2R 0DX.

Shipley, J., *Starting Technology 1 and 2*, Holmes McDougall, Allander House, 137–141 Leith Walk, Edinburgh EH6 8NS

Stanley Tools, Woodside, Sheffield, S3 9PD.

Studies in Design Education, Craft and Technology, 151 Etruria Road, Hanley, Stoke-on-Trent.

Technology Supplies, 6 Stoke Court, Stoke on Tern, Market Drayton, Shropshire TF9 2DY.

Timber Research and Development Association, Hughendon Valley, High Wycombe, Bucks. HP14 4ND.

Trylon Ltd, Thrift Street, Wollaston, Northants NN9 7QJ.

Williams, P., and Jinks, D., *Design and Technology 5–12*, Falmer Press, Rankine Road, Basingstoke, Hampshire RG24 0PR.

Illustration 4.3

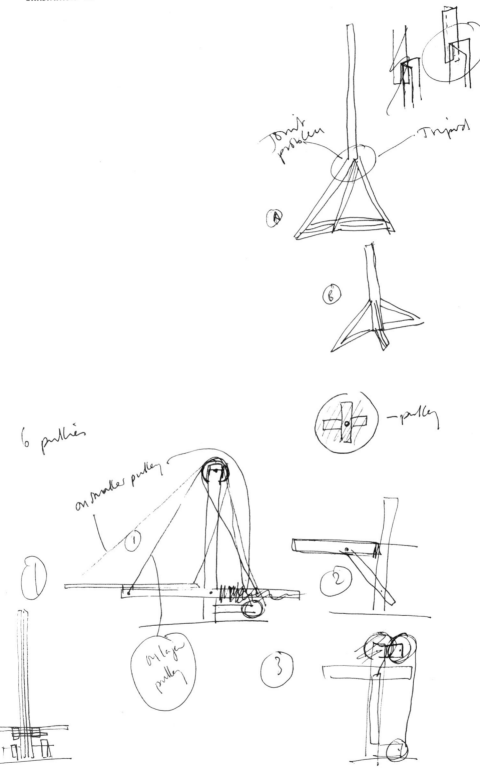

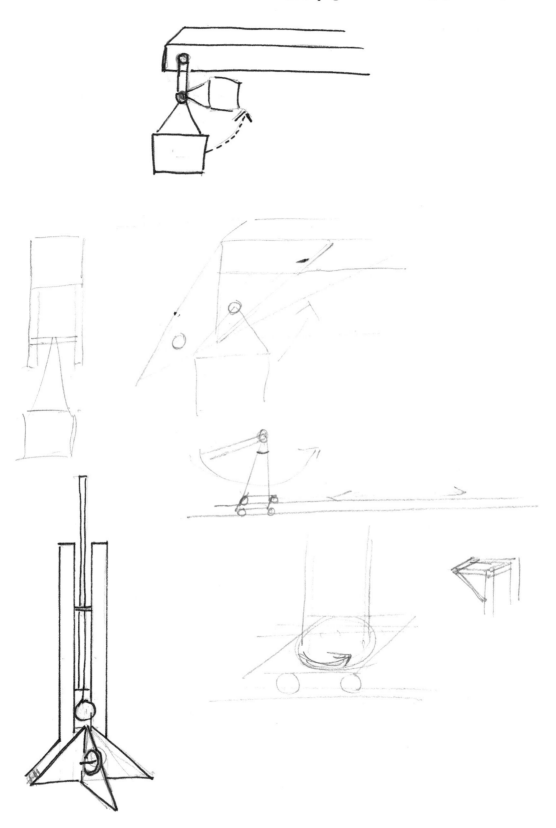

(iii) Further details for lifting devices

(iv) Completed lifting devices

The lifting mechanisms by Mark Devereux and Eric Marshall (Illustration 4.3) provide further examples of this combination of considerations — thought processes to solve the problem of producing a lifting device capable of lifting a given load to a specified height; initial ideas about structures crudely sketched (showing contrast to the finished drawings of the earlier examples); choice of materials; use of cutting and joining skills; modifications to structures to ensure stability and to mechanisms to effect efficiency; testing of the devices; and the introduction of coloured plastic for both mechanical and aesthetic purposes.

Much less complex are the examples by the same teachers of the use of plastic materials (Illustrations 4.4a and b, and 4.5). In this case plastics were unfamiliar to them in the context of designing and making. Polystyrene, a familiar material, provided experience with a semi-resistant material with design potential, but with severe health and safety risks if it gives off fumes by burning. In this case the task: *to design and sculpt an animal in polystyrene* was followed by a set of instructions on how to translate drawings into 'working drawings', and then into cardboard templates. A demonstration of pinning a template to the material, and the safe use of a hot-wire-cutter, provided the information necessary for the solutions to be reached at the same time as new skills were acquired.

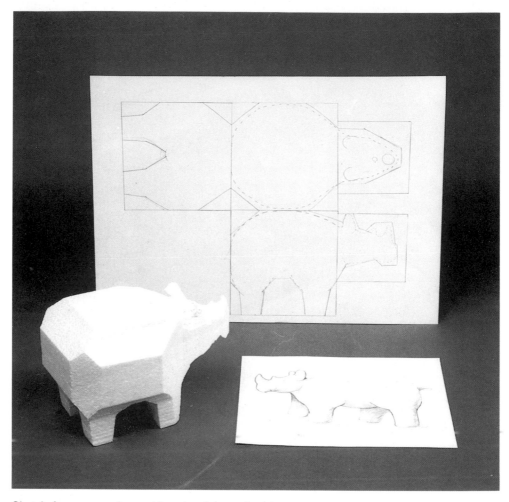

Sketch from research, working drawing, and sculpture

Similar procedures with another unfamiliar material and piece of equipment were followed in the presentation of a further design brief: *to produce a desk-top work-card stand made from acrylic sheet (maximum size 200 × 100 mm) using an electric stripheater.* A major difference in this project is that the design drawings were translated first into cardboard prototypes, whereby several different ideas could be viewed and partly tested in less expensive material first. By using this step in the procedures the problem of then translating from prototype materials to final product also had to be taken into account. An important similarity between the two projects using plastics is that both required a session of materials-testing, using off-cuts. Those sessions provided some prior knowledge and skill which could then be applied.

The presentation and conduct of each of these projects incorporated a range of teaching strategies. Problem-solving activities can involve the teacher and/or the pupils in any of the types of teaching/learning activities in the classroom shown in Table 4.2.

Judgments about which teaching strategies may be appropriate for particular pupils or

Illustration 4.4b

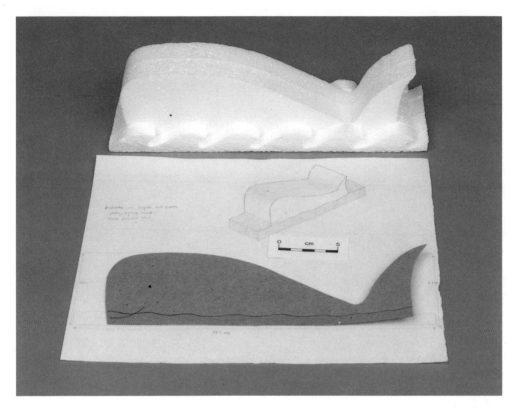

Drawing, template and sculpture

projects need to be made by individual teachers. In the examples above we have tried to indicate points at which new skills and knowledge were introduced, working within procedures in which decision-making and problem-solving were left to individuals.

In the examples using plastics it is clear that the limitations on the tasks were severe, and the teaching strategy largely didactic and instructional. In the earlier ones the tasks set and teaching strategies used involved rather less instruction, and greater freedom to pursue ideas. There has been considerable debate about the appropriateness and place of didactic instruction, and the major tensions between that and 'freer' approaches to problem-solving have been considered elsewhere (Schools Council, 1974; Tickle, 1983; DES, 1983). The issues surrounding that tension and the dilemmas which it brings for teachers also form a theme in the later chapters of this book. In the following section, Eric Marshall takes account of those issues in devising a series of lessons in technology, focusing on structures and forces. This example illustrates the acquisition of CDT experience and the translation of knowledge, skills, attitudes, and values into specific teaching proposals. This stage of planning for teaching is as complex as the range of knowledge to be acquired and incorporated into teaching. In this instance the judgments made about which knowledge pupils are assumed to have, which to introduce, and how to develop opportunities for the application of knowledge through practical experience are all taken into consideration for planning a series of learning experiences.

Illustration 4.5

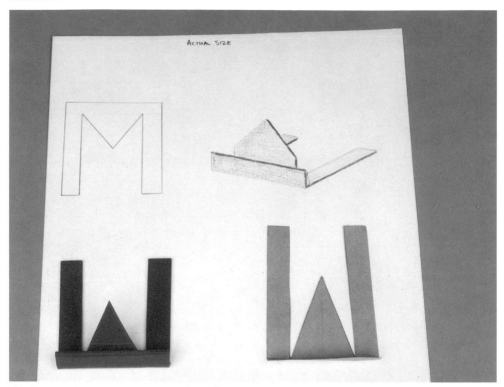

(i) Drawings, card prototype, and product

(ii) Other solutions: acrylic sheet work-card supports

Table 4.2: Range of Possible Teaching/Learning Activities

information-giving	instruction
demonstration	practical experience with tools/equipment
guided questioning	group discussion
perusing sources for ideas	displays
direction of formal safety requirements	
testing of products and recording results	
experimenting with materials	
problem-posing	

Structures and Forces: A series of lessons for children aged 10–11

The central aims of this series of activities are:

1. To consolidate and develop further a range of design, craft and general learning skills:

Design skills
working to a design brief;
following the design process;
observation as part of investigation;
recording, analyzing, interpreting, presenting data;
considering and choosing from options;
constructing working models;
devising and administering a 'fair test';

Craft skills
using simple craft tools (knives, scissors, etc.);
manipulation of craft materials (card, balsa wood, etc.);
making and using templates (a new skill);
using a hot-wire-cutter on polystyrene (a new skill);

General learning
planning, organizing and carrying out a group task;
following written instructions;
report writing.

2. To consolidate and develop further knowledge and understanding of structures and forces, specifically:

properties of materials as a design consideration;
strength/weight ratio as a property of materials;

forces at work on structures and the terms used to describe them;
geometric shapes as structural properties.

Learning is presented in four stages, starting from first-hand knowledge of design in the environment, proceeding to an introduction of concepts and associated language, an exploration of the properties of structures, and the production of solutions to a design problem.

Stage One uses designed objects to draw out from the pupils some aspects of the relationship between design, materials and forces through observation and discussion.

Stage Two examines these forces in detail through demonstrations and practical activities to show how forces can determine choice of design materials.

Stage Three explores various structures used to exploit the inherent strength of materials.

Stage Four provides a design brief which requires the production of the highest possible structure to support the greatest possible load, while spanning a gap 50 cm wide, using card, balsa wood or polystyrene.

Lesson 1: A pack of photographs (or colour slides) is used to look analytically at a range of common objects within the children's experience (see Illustration 4.6). This highlights the impact of design (natural and human) and designers on our surroundings. Questions stimulate discussion about the considerations and constraints which influence designs. Specifically discussion is centred upon the identification of needs or problems, and the selection of suitable materials to meet/solve the need/problem. Within that, account is taken of the forces which act upon objects when in use. Initial questions concern the needs which prompted a design (or evolution of a natural object) and the functions the objects serve, such as: door jambs and lintel, bicycle (support); snail shell (protection); egg (enclosure, mobility, penetrability); bridge crane (span and support); honeycomb (enclosure, accessibility, efficient use of space).

Discussion about whether such objects and others serve their function adequately and are designed efficiently follow from the description and analysis of the features and purposes of the items photographed. In particular, questions about the kinds of forces which act upon the structures, and ways they serve to meet those forces, are considered.

Lesson 2: Consideration of forces which act upon structures and which they need to resist (or sometimes assist, as with a chick breaking out of an egg or an element of 'give' in a bridge) is continued and elaborated. The choice of materials to make designs which can at least support their own weight and resist the force of gravity is introduced. Further, the idea that most structures additionally need to support other loads or resist other forces is critical to choice of materials.

Demonstration: a skeletal cube made of drinking straws maintains its shape against gravity. It is thus far a successful structure. However it cannot support the load of a book, where load and force of gravity upon it combine to squash the structure.

Discussion: what other kinds of loads and forces do other structures need to contend with?

Following presentations from pupils represented in their own terms, concepts and specialist terms are introduced through activity: COMPRESSION is demonstrated by pupils squatting on the floor, learning forward to take their weight on their hands until balanced and supported by arms only. Pressure on arms, wrists and elbows results from them being *compressed* under the weight of their own bodies, and the supporting force exerted by the floor. Pupils

Illustration 4.6

Figure 4.1: Compression

seek other examples in the classroom of structures under compression — tables, the walls of the building, bookcases, etc.

Further demonstration of the effects of excessive compression loads, and the effects of different materials in resisting the forces are given. Tasks which enable the pupils to test different loads, materials and structures provide practical experience. Suitable visual records are produced to reinforce the concepts and language, and to help later recall.

Figure 4.2: Tension

Lesson 3: Following recall and reiteration, similar procedures are used to introduce the concept of TENSION. Demonstration is achieved by asking two pupils to lift a PE bench with straight arms, with a third pupil sitting mid-way along it. The stretching of the muscles is caused by the weight (force of gravity) acting against the resistant muscular force of the arms. Examples of structures in tension around the school are sought and considered.

Practical work testing the effects of different tension loads on materials, and the tensile strength of them, follows: threads, elastic bands, chain, etc., leading to practical applications of the concepts involved, and recording of observations. Supplementary visual aids extend the classroom record of the project.

Lesson 4: Similar procedures are followed to demonstrate, explain, and experience the notion of SHEAR forces and torsion where loads acting in opposite directions result in materials being sliced, cut, or twisted. The action of scissors cutting paper or cloth, of a guillotine, or of hedging shears, provide everyday examples of shear force. Such obvious and 'excessive' examples (i.e. leading to change in the material) lead to consideration of less obvious and often unnoticed cases of shear force: items fixed to walls with brackets and screws, such as fire

Figure 4.3: Shear

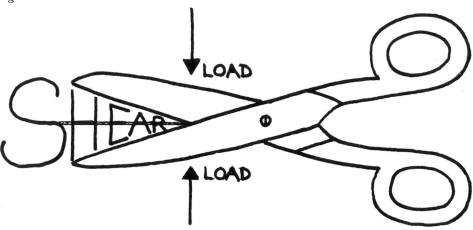

extinguishers, radiators, etc., are used to show the 'hidden' existence of shear force, and to consider the design and use of appropriate fixing mechanisms.

Lesson 5: With experience of loads and forces, extension is gained by considering STATIC and DYNAMIC loads, and the ways in which structures can experience different kinds of loads and forces at different times. An introduction to the idea of static loads is made by recalling that objects carry their own weight — a relatively unchanging load. Additional steady loads are carried by walls, beams, and (relatively) tables. These examples are contrasted with sudden, changing and dynamic loads upon floorboards, window panes (resisting wind pressure), car tyres, railway tracks, felt-tip pens, and fairground rides.

Figure 4.4: Dynamic/Static

Demonstration of static and dynamic loads is achieved by returning to the PE bench demonstration. The child sitting still in the centre of the bench produces tension in the arms of those holding the bench. Standing up and sitting down releases and reimposes part of the load, producing different impacts on the muscles.

Consideration of different kinds of structures which experience dynamic forces leads to analysis of some which may need to cope with compression, tension, and shear forces, either static or dynamic or both, thus bringing the concepts together in application and analysis. Demonstration is provided by using a sheet of thick card with two pins in each side, and thread stretched across the pins. A 'bridge' is made by placing the card flat across two blocks. A load is applied by pressing in the middle of the card. Compression in the upper surface is indicated by slackening of the thread, tension in the lower surface by tightening of the thread. Photographs used in Lesson 1 are returned to, for reconsideration to identify additional characteristics which were not noticed earlier, in the light of these lessons.

Figure 4.5: Multiple Forces

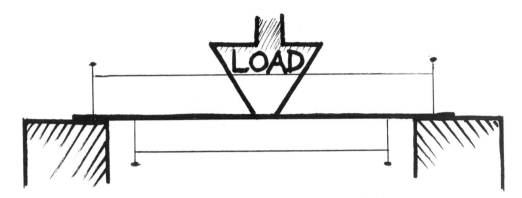

Further practical work on STRENGTH IN SHAPES IN STRUCTURES is introduced to a groups of pupils, through the use of work-cards. These encourage cooperation in observation and discussion, in the use of ideas and construction of objects. The first sheet gives an introduction to building structures. Extension work follows to provide deeper understanding of structural principles and a chance to develop modified forms and to test them.

Strength, Weight and Reinforcement — Notes

The objective is to demonstrate the value of reinforcement as a means of increasing the rigidity of a material and thus increasing its value as a building material. A further objective is to explore 'efficient' — i.e. the lightest and strongest forms of reinforcement.

The best shape for a reinforcing rib made from card is perhaps a T shape produced by folding the card as shown in Figure 4.6.

Figure 4.6: Reinforcing rib

Groups are encouraged to explore the effects of making longer and shorter 'legs' in the reinforcing shapes. This links with the work on beams. The idea of reinforcement can be extended to discuss reinforced concrete, or the use of selective reinforcement of weak spots, to achieve economic use of materials.

STRENGTH AND WEIGHT

YOU WILL NEED:—

BALANCE TO WEIGH
TO NEAREST 0.5 GRAM
TWO BLOCKS OF WOOD
5-GRAM WEIGHTS
CRAFT KNIFE
FILE
LENGTHS OF POLYSTYRENE BLOCK
THICK CARD
BALSA WOOD SHEET
THIN PLASTIC SHEET

① USING THE CORRECT TOOL (CRAFT KNIFE OR FILE) TRIM THE PIECES OF WOOD, CARD ETC UNTIL THEY WEIGH 15 GRAMS

TRY TO KEEP THE PIECES THE SAME LENGTH IF YOU CAN

② NOW COPY OUT THE FOLLOWING CHART

MATERIAL (WEIGHT: 15grams)	LOAD CARRIED BEFORE COLLAPSING

③ RECORD THE NAME ON THE CHART OF THE MATERIAL YOU ARE TESTING

④ PUT THE WOOD-BLOCKS 8 cm. APART AND USE THE FIRST PIECE OF MATERIAL TO BE TESTED TO MAKE A BRIDGE AS SHOWN IN THE DIAGRAM.

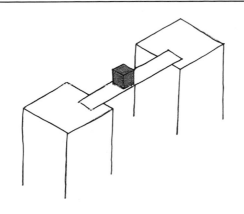

⑤ NOW LOAD THE
5-GRAM WEIGHTS ON
TOP OF THE BRIDGE AS
SHOWN IN THE DIAGRAM
UNTIL IT COLLAPSES OR
SNAPS

NOTE DOWN ON THE
CHART THE LOAD IT
COULD CARRY BEFORE IT
SNAPPED OR COLLAPSED

TEST THE OTHER MATERIALS IN THE SAME WAY

WHICH MATERIAL CARRIED THE BIGGEST LOAD?

EACH MATERIAL CAN CARRY A LOAD.
THIS LOAD IS HOW MANY TIMES HEAVIER
THAN THE MATERIAL ITSELF?

THIS IS CALLED A MATERIALS
"STRENGTH TO WEIGHT RATIO"

WHICH IS THE STRONGEST MATERIAL?

STRENGTH IN SHAPES

REINFORCEMENT

YOU WILL NEED :—

SHEETS OF CARD   GLUE
2 WOODEN BLOCKS   PENCIL
5-GRAM WEIGHTS   RULER.
SCISSORS

① MAKE A BRIDGE USING TWO
WOODEN BLOCKS AND A SHEET OF
CARD AS SHOWN IN DIAGRAM Ⓐ

LOAD THE BRIDGE WITH 5-GRAM
WEIGHTS UNTIL IT COLLAPSES.

HOW MUCH WEIGHT COULD IT
SUPPORT ?

DIAGRAM Ⓐ

NOW MAKE AN 'L'-SHAPED
STRIP AND GLUE IT TO THE
BACK OF THE CARD, AS SHOWN
IN DIAGRAM Ⓑ

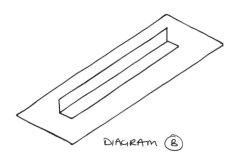

DIAGRAM Ⓑ

TEST THE CARD BRIDGE AGAIN.

CAN IT CARRY MORE WEIGHT?

WHY DOES THE CARD STRIP
MAKE THE BRIDGE STRONGER?

WHAT DOES THE CARD STRIP
HELP TO DO WHEN THE BRIDGE
IS CARRYING A LOAD?

HOW CAN YOU MAKE THE BRIDGE EVEN STRONGER USING ONLY
STRIPS OF CARD?

IS THE 'L'-SHAPED STRIP THE BEST SHAPE FOR A REINFORCING STRIP?

IS IT THE STRONGEST SHAPE? INVENT AND TEST SOME OTHER SHAPES.

WOULD A FRAMEWORK OF STRIPS UNDERNEATH THE CARD MAKE THE BRIDGE EVEN STRONGER?

TEST SOME DIFFERENT KINDS OF FRAMEWORKS, LIKE THOSE SHOWN IN DIAGRAM Ⓒ

RECORD THE RESULTS OF YOUR INVESTIGATIONS

WHICH KIND OF FRAMEWORK GIVES THE GREATEST STRENGTH?

DIAGRAM Ⓒ

MAKE THE STRONGEST CARD BRIDGE YOU CAN, USING CARD STRIPS TO REINFORCE IT

HOW MUCH WEIGHT CAN IT SUPPORT?

Strength in Shapes: Beams — Notes

The objective is to demonstrate how the inherent strength of a material can be exploited by changing its shape. A further objective is to allow pupils to explore how loads act upon beams.

Beams under load are subject to compression on the upper edge/surface and tension on the lower. Buckling along the top edge of the card beams is due in part to cardboard's lack of rigidity. If the edge is given added rigidity by gluing on a strip of card this greatly increases the strength of the beam: hence the shape of steel girders. The strength of a beam is proportional to its height, provided the material in the middle is sufficiently strong to withstand the load. Unfortunately cardboard has limited rigidity, so beyond a certain height the strength of the beam will begin to drop off again. More able children might plot the strength/height relationship.

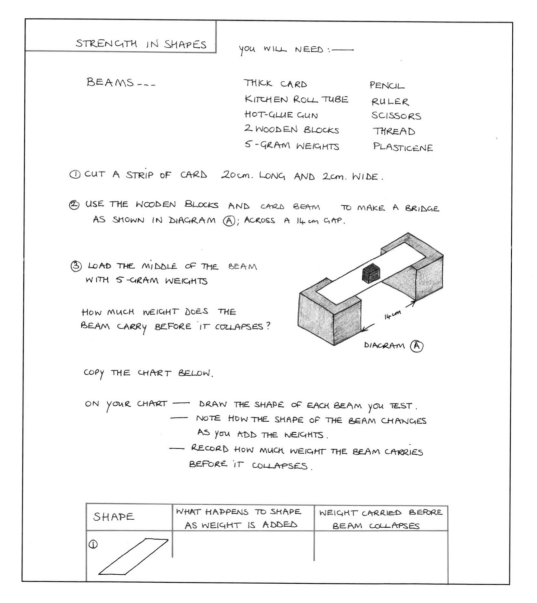

STRENGTH IN SHAPES

YOU WILL NEED :—

BEAMS ---

THICK CARD   PENCIL
KITCHEN ROLL TUBE   RULER
HOT-GLUE GUN   SCISSORS
2 WOODEN BLOCKS   THREAD
5-GRAM WEIGHTS   PLASTICENE

① CUT A STRIP OF CARD 20cm. LONG AND 2cm. WIDE.

② USE THE WOODEN BLOCKS AND CARD BEAM TO MAKE A BRIDGE AS SHOWN IN DIAGRAM Ⓐ; ACROSS A 14cm GAP.

③ LOAD THE MIDDLE OF THE BEAM WITH 5-GRAM WEIGHTS

HOW MUCH WEIGHT DOES THE BEAM CARRY BEFORE IT COLLAPSES?

14cm

DIAGRAM Ⓐ

COPY THE CHART BELOW.

ON YOUR CHART —— DRAW THE SHAPE OF EACH BEAM YOU TEST.
—— NOTE HOW THE SHAPE OF THE BEAM CHANGES AS YOU ADD THE WEIGHTS.
—— RECORD HOW MUCH WEIGHT THE BEAM CARRIES BEFORE IT COLLAPSES.

SHAPE	WHAT HAPPENS TO SHAPE AS WEIGHT IS ADDED	WEIGHT CARRIED BEFORE BEAM COLLAPSES
①		

④ NOW CUT A 20cm LONG, 2cm WIDE CARD STRIP
STAND THIS STRIP ON ITS EDGE AND FIX IT FIRMLY WITH PLASTICENE
AS SHOWN IN DIAGRAM Ⓑ

⑤ USING THREAD, HANG THE
WEIGHTS UNDERNEATH THE BEAM

⑥ LOOK AT THE TOP EDGE OF THE
BEAM AS YOU ADD THE WEIGHTS.

WHAT HAPPENS TO IT?

DIAGRAM Ⓑ

⑦ HOW MUCH WEIGHT DOES THIS BEAM CARRY BEFORE IT COLLAPSES?

IS IT STRONGER THAN THE WIDE BEAM?
WHY DOES IT HAVE MORE STRENGTH THAN THE WIDE BEAM?

WHY DID THE TOP EDGE BEGIN TO BUCKLE AS YOU ADDED THE WEIGHTS?

IF YOU STOP THE TOP EDGE BUCKLING, DO YOU THINK IT WILL MAKE THE
BEAM STRONGER?

⑧ CUT A NEW 20cm × 2cm CARD STRIP.
GLUE A 1cm WIDE STRIP ALONG THE TOP EDGE, AS IN DIAGRAM Ⓒ.
NOW TEST THE BEAM.

IS THIS BEAM STRONGER? WHY IS IT STRONGER?

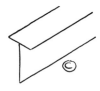 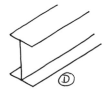 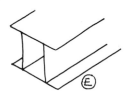 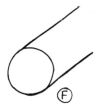

⑨ NOW MAKE AND TEST THE SHAPES Ⓓ, Ⓔ AND Ⓕ
MAKE A LIST SHOWING THE STRONGEST BEAM FIRST AND THE WEAKEST LAST.
CAN YOU EXPLAIN WHY SOME BEAMS ARE STRONGER THAN OTHERS?
DOES THE GAP BETWEEN THE WOODEN BLOCKS AFFECT THE STRENGTH OF THE BEAMS?

STRENGTH IN SHAPES

YOU WILL NEED:——

THICK CARD	PENCIL
HOT-GLUE GUN	RULER
2 WOODEN BLOCKS	SCISSORS
5-GRAM WEIGHTS	THREAD

MORE BEAMS.....

DOES THE <u>WIDTH</u> OF THE STRIPS ON THE TOP AND BOTTOM OF A BEAM AFFECT ITS STRENGTH?

MAKE SOME BEAMS WITH WIDER AND NARROWER STRIPS TO FIND OUT...

DOES THE <u>HEIGHT</u> OF A BEAM AFFECT ITS STRENGTH?

MAKE A BEAM 3cm TALL AND 20cm LONG, AS SHOWN IN DIAGRAM Ⓐ

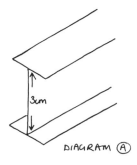

3cm

DIAGRAM Ⓐ

TEST THIS BEAM.
CAN IT SUPPORT MORE WEIGHT THAN THE OTHER BEAMS YOU HAVE TESTED?

MAKE SOME TALLER BEAMS—SAY 3.5cm, 4cm AND 4.5cm TALL. TEST THEM.

ARE TALLER BEAMS ALWAYS STRONGER?

WHAT IS THE HEIGHT OF THE STRONGEST BEAM YOU CAN MAKE FROM THICK CARD?

WHY ARE THE TALLEST BEAMS MADE FROM CARD WEAK?

NOW MAKE AND TEST SOME TALL BOX-BEAMS AS SHOWN IN DIAGRAM Ⓑ

HOW MUCH WEIGHT CAN YOUR STRONGEST BOX-BEAM SUPPORT?

WHY IS A BOX-BEAM STRONGER THAN AN "I"-SHAPED BEAM?

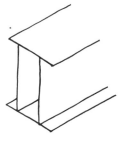

DIAGRAM Ⓑ

FIND SOME PICTURES OF STEEL BEAMS.

WHERE ARE THE THICKEST PARTS OF THE BEAM?

WHY DO SOME BEAMS HAVE HOLES IN THE MIDDLE SECTION?

WHAT DOES THIS TELL YOU ABOUT WHERE THE FORCE ACTS ON A BEAM WHEN A LOAD IS PLACED ON IT?

Strength in Shapes: Pillars — Notes

The objective is to demonstrate the action of forces on pillars, and the ways in which loads are carried by different forms of hollow pillar.

The first sheet demonstrates that a cylindrical form is the best for a pillar. The second attempts to show how loads act upon different shapes of pillars. This would perhaps only suit the most able pupils, with supporting discussion. Putting slits in the side of the square and triangular pillars has little effect on their strength, since the bulk of the load is carried by the rigid corners. The cylindrical pillar shows that the load is carried by all the material, as it collapses into a 'Chinese lantern' shape when the load is added. On the other hand, putting notches in the corners of the square and triangular pillars reduces their strength markedly, while rows of notches in the cylinder makes less impact on its strength.

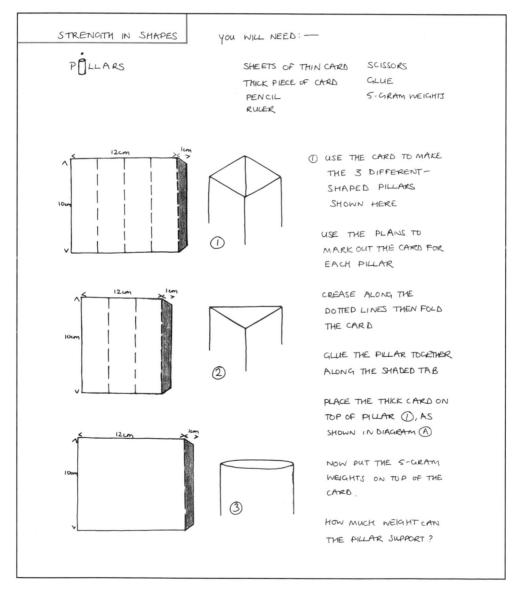

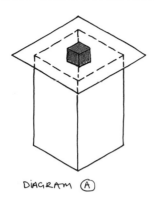

DIAGRAM Ⓐ

COPY THE CHART BELOW

ON THE CHART —

① SKETCH THE SHAPE OF THE PILLAR YOU TESTED.

② NOTE DOWN HOW MUCH WEIGHT IT CARRIED BEFORE COLLAPSING

SHAPE	HOW MUCH WEIGHT CARRIED
①	

MAKE A LIST SHOWING THE STRONGEST SHAPE FIRST AND THE WEAKEST LAST

WHY DO YOU THINK BONES HAVE A HOLLOW TUBE-SHAPE?

STRENGTH IN SHAPES

MORE P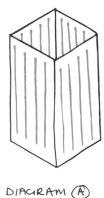LLARS

YOU WILL NEED :—

SHEETS OF THIN CARD   PENCIL
THICK PIECE OF CARD   RULER
CRAFT KNIFE   SCISSORS
5-GRAM WEIGHTS   GLUE

① USE THE PLANS FROM THE PREVIOUS SHEET TO MAKE A NEW SET OF DIFFERENT-SHAPED PILLARS.

✳ THIS TIME, PUT A NUMBER OF SLITS IN THE <u>SIDES</u> OF THE PILLARS USING THE CRAFT KNIFE, AS SHOWN IN DIAGRAM Ⓐ

NOW TEST TO SEE HOW MUCH WEIGHT THE PILLARS CAN SUPPORT.

DIAGRAM Ⓐ

DO THE SLITS IN THE SIDES AFFECT THE STRENGTH OF ALL THE PILLARS ?

WHICH IS THE WEAKEST PILLAR ?
WHAT HAPPENS TO THE SHAPE OF THE WEAKEST PILLAR WHEN YOU PUT WEIGHTS ON THE TOP?

DO THE SLOTS IN THE SIDES OF THE TRIANGULAR AND SQUARE PILLARS HAVE A BIG EFFECT ON THEIR STRENGTH? WHY NOT?

② MAKE ANOTHER SET OF PILLARS

✳ THIS TIME PUT A ROW OF NOTCHES DOWN THE <u>CORNERS</u> OF THE SQUARE AND TRIANGULAR PILLARS, AS IN DIAGRAM Ⓑ
PUT 4 LINES OF NOTCHES DOWN THE SIDE OF THE ROUND PILLAR.

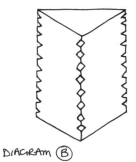

DIAGRAM Ⓑ

NOW TEST THESE PILLARS

WHICH IS THE STRONGEST PILLAR NOW?

WHICH IS THE WEAKEST PILLAR?

CAN YOU THINK WHY HOLES IN THE CORNERS OF THE TRIANGULAR AND SQUARE PILLARS CHANGE THEIR STRENGTH A LOT?

WHERE DO YOU THINK MOST OF THE LOAD IS CARRIED IN PILLARS WHICH ARE TRIANGULAR OR SQUARE?

HOW COULD YOU MAKE A TRIANGULAR OR SQUARE PILLAR STRONGER?

WHERE DO YOU THINK THE LOAD IS CARRIED IN A ROUND PILLAR?

WHY IS A ROUND PILLAR USUALLY STRONGER-?

STRENGTH IN SHAPES

TEST THE STRENGTH
OF THESE SHAPES :—

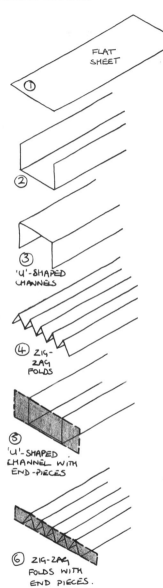

① FLAT SHEET

② 'U'-SHAPED CHANNELS

③

④ ZIG-ZAG FOLDS

⑤ 'U'-SHAPED CHANNEL WITH END-PIECES

⑥ ZIG-ZAG FOLDS WITH END PIECES.

YOU WILL NEED :—

7 PIECES OF CARD (7 x 15 cm)
5-GRAM WEIGHTS
2 BLOCKS OF WOOD
SCISSORS
GLUE
RULER

① MAKE A BRIDGE BETWEEN THE TWO BLOCKS OF WOOD USING THE SHEET OF CARD, AS SHOWN IN THE DIAGRAM BELOW.

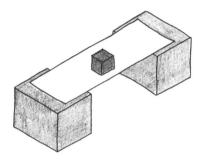

② LOAD THE MIDDLE OF THE BRIDGE WITH THE 5-GRAM WEIGHTS, ONE AT A TIME, AS SHOWN IN THE DIAGRAM.

WHAT HAPPENS TO THE SHAPE OF THE BRIDGE AS YOU ADD THE WEIGHTS?

HOW MUCH WEIGHT WILL THE BRIDGE CARRY BEFORE IT COLLAPSES?

COPY OUT THE CHART SHOWN BELOW

ON YOUR CHART —— DRAW THE SHAPE OF THE CARD YOU USE.

—— NOTE DOWN WHAT HAPPENS TO THE SHAPE AS YOU ADD THE WEIGHTS.

—— RECORD HOW MUCH WEIGHT THE SHAPE CARRIED BEFORE IT COLLAPSED.

SHAPE	WHAT HAPPENED TO SHAPE AS WEIGHT ADDED	WEIGHT CARRIED BEFORE COLLAPSING
①		

REPEAT THE SAME TEST FOR SHAPES ① TO ④.

CAN YOU SUGGEST REASONS WHY SOME SHAPES CAN CARRY MORE WEIGHT THAN OTHERS?

TEST SHAPES ⑤ AND ⑥. WHICH IS THE STRONGEST?

MAKE A LIST OF ALL THE SHAPES. SHOW THE STRONGEST FIRST AND THE WEAKEST LAST.

HOW COULD YOU MAKE SHAPES ⑤ AND ⑥ EVEN STRONGER?

COULD YOU MAKE SHAPES ⑤ AND ⑥ LIGHTER YET STILL KEEP THE SAME STRENGTH?

INVENT SOME CARD SHAPES OF YOUR OWN AND TEST THEIR STRENGTH.

Strength in Shapes: Triangles — Notes

The objective is to demonstrate that a triangle is a 'naturally rigid' structure, and that it can be used as a means of keeping other shapes rigid.

The first sheet introduces the 'naturally rigid' triangle and the use of triangular forms. The second sheet makes practical use of that knowledge. The cube needs to be as large a possible, so large-format newspapers are needed. Bracing struts are added corner to corner. Shorter struts could be used by bracing the corners.

The drinking-straw beams need to be carefully constructed and built using the same kind of joints to the same standard. The joints need to be butted to get the greatest strength from the straws. Two side frames should be produced first, then joined by cross-members. Pins can hold these together while glue is applied.

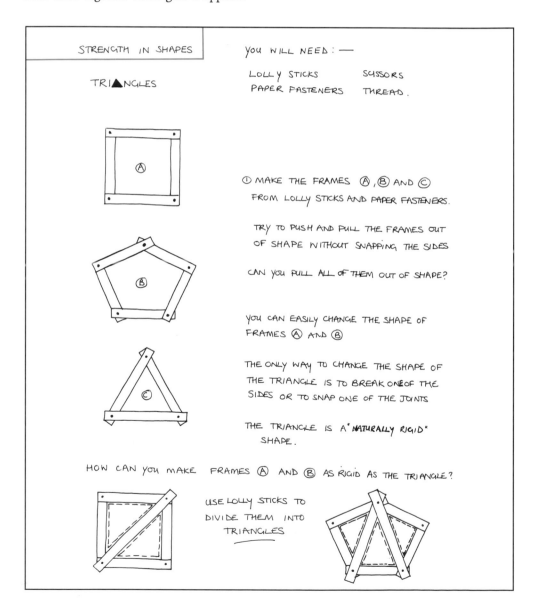

② MAKE THE FRAME SHOWN IN DIAGRAM ⒟ FROM LOLLY STICKS AND PAPER FASTENERS.

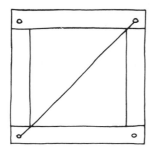

DIAGRAM ⒟

FIX A PIECE OF THREAD DIAGONALLY ACROSS THE FRAME

THIS THREAD TAKES THE PLACE OF A LOLLY STICK.

NOW <u>GENTLY</u> PULL THE FRAME OUT OF SHAPE

<u>DON'T</u> SNAP THE THREAD.

WHAT HAPPENS TO THE THREAD?

WHAT KIND OF FORCE ACTS ON THE THREAD?

IS IT IN 'TENSION' (BEING PULLED)?

OR IS IT IN COMPRESSION (BEING SQUASHED)?

NOW PULL THE FRAME THE OTHER WAY.

WHAT HAPPENS TO THE THREAD NOW?
WHAT KIND OF FORCE IS ACTING ON IT?

LOOK AT DIAGRAM ⒠

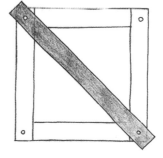

DIAGRAM ⒠

THE SHADED CROSS-PIECE KEEPS THE WHOLE FRAME RIGID.

WHAT SORT OF FORCES WILL THE CROSS-PIECE NEED TO RESIST IN ORDER TO KEEP THE WHOLE FRAME RIGID IF YOU TRY TO PULL OR PUSH IT OUT OF SHAPE?

STRENGTH IN SHAPES

YOU WILL NEED :—

TRIANGLES

DRINKING STRAWS   SCISSORS

NEWSPAPERS   HOT-GLUE GUN

SHEET OF STIFF CARD   KILOGRAM WEIGHTS

MASKING TAPE   5-GRAM WEIGHTS

① MAKE THE TUBULAR CUBE SHOWN IN DIAGRAM Ⓐ

MAKE THE TUBES FROM TIGHTLY-ROLLED
SHEETS OF NEWSPAPER, BOUND WITH
MASKING-TAPE

GLUE THE TUBES TOGETHER TO
MAKE THE CUBE WITH THE HOT-GLUE
GUN

MAKE SURE THE JOINTS ARE
STRONGLY MADE

PLACE THE SHEET OF CARDBOARD
ON TOP OF THE CUBE

NOW START TO ADD THE WEIGHTS

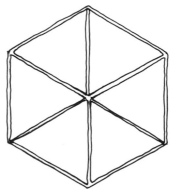

DIAGRAM Ⓐ

HOW MUCH WEIGHT WILL THE CUBE SUPPORT BEFORE IT BEGINS
TO BUCKLE ?

HOW CAN YOU MAKE THE CUBE STRONGER ?

IF YOU ADD CROSS-STRUTS TO THE FOUR SIDES OF THE CUBE, AS IN
DIAGRAM Ⓑ, DO THEY MAKE THE CUBE STRONGER ?

DIAGRAM Ⓑ

WHY SHOULD THE CROSS-STRUTS MAKE THE
CUBE STRONGER?

WHERE ELSE CAN YOU PUT CROSS-STRUTS TO
MAKE THE CUBE STRONGER?

CAN YOU MAKE THE STRUTS AS SHORT AS
POSSIBLE, YET KEEP THE SAME STRENGTH?

① NOW USING THE HOT-GLUE GUN, MAKE
THE GIRDERS SHOWN IN THE DIAGRAMS
Ⓒ AND Ⓓ FROM DRINKING STRAWS

MAKE THEM AS CAREFULLY AND
ACCURATELY AS POSSIBLE

WHICH DO YOU THINK WILL BE
THE STRONGER GIRDER?

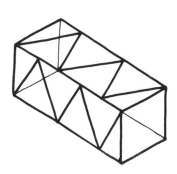

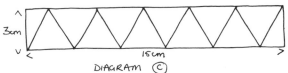

3cm

15cm

DIAGRAM Ⓒ

TO TEST THE GIRDERS MAKE A
BRIDGE WITH EACH ONE AND LOAD
THE 5-GRAM WEIGHTS ON TOP

HOW COULD YOU MAKE A GIRDER
WHICH IS STRONGER AND
LIGHTER?

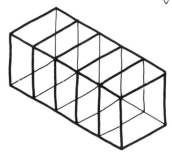

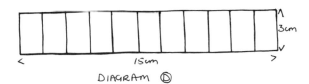

3cm

15cm

DIAGRAM Ⓓ

Strength in Shapes: Arches — Notes

The objective is to develop understanding of how an arch structure works and how it reacts under a load; the need for abutments; the need for stability by other means. A further objective is to demonstrate how structure affects the load-bearing capacity of a material by comparing the load carried by a beam with that carried by an arch of the same material covering the same span.

The arch exploits the strength of stone, polystyrene, balsa wood, etc., when in compression. A discussion is held about how 'real-life' arches are erected, and the need for supporting frameworks during construction, until a keystone is fitted. The second sheet is less structured and requires the group to work more independently, planning the assembly of the balsa wood arch. The arch can be tied using card (as a rigid tie) or strips (as a flexible tie) to give it greater stability. When ties have been added discussion could turn to arch suspension bridges such as Sydney Harbour or Runcorn, and how they work.

Craft skills such as the use of hot-glue-gun and hot-wire-cutter require re-emphasis on safety rules.

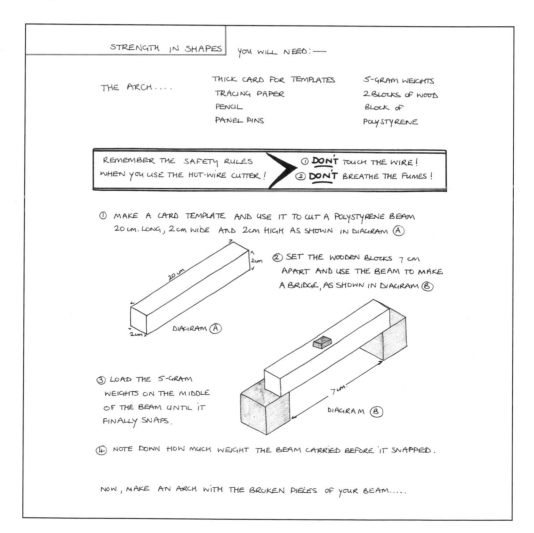

STRENGTH IN SHAPES

YOU WILL NEED:—

THE ARCH....

THICK CARD FOR TEMPLATES
TRACING PAPER
PENCIL
PANEL PINS

5-GRAM WEIGHTS
2 BLOCKS OF WOOD
BLOCK OF
POLYSTYRENE

REMEMBER THE SAFETY RULES WHEN YOU USE THE HOT-WIRE CUTTER!

① **DON'T** TOUCH THE WIRE!
② **DON'T** BREATHE THE FUMES!

① MAKE A CARD TEMPLATE AND USE IT TO CUT A POLYSTYRENE BEAM 20 cm. LONG, 2 cm WIDE AND 2 cm HIGH AS SHOWN IN DIAGRAM Ⓐ

② SET THE WOODEN BLOCKS 7 cm APART AND USE THE BEAM TO MAKE A BRIDGE, AS SHOWN IN DIAGRAM Ⓑ

DIAGRAM Ⓐ

③ LOAD THE 5-GRAM WEIGHTS ON THE MIDDLE OF THE BEAM UNTIL IT FINALLY SNAPS.

DIAGRAM Ⓑ

④ NOTE DOWN HOW MUCH WEIGHT THE BEAM CARRIED BEFORE IT SNAPPED.

NOW, MAKE AN ARCH WITH THE BROKEN PIECES OF YOUR BEAM.....

① TRACE THIS SHAPE.

MAKE A CARD TEMPLATE FROM IT.

② USE THE TEMPLATE TO MAKE 9 BLOCKS FROM THE PIECES OF YOUR BEAM.

THE 9 PIECES MAKE AN ARCH WHICH SPANS A 7cm. GAP LIKE THE BEAM DID IN THE FIRST EXPERIMENT

DIAGRAM Ⓒ

③ PUT A 5-GRAM WEIGHT ON THE TOP OF THE ARCH, ON THE BLOCK WHICH IS SHADED IN DIAGRAM Ⓒ.

WHAT HAPPENS TO THE ARCH?

WHY DO THE BLOCKS MOVE?

HOW CAN YOU STOP THE BLOCKS MOVING?

④ PUT THE ARCH BACK TOGETHER.

THIS TIME PUT A HEAVY BOOK AT EACH END OF THE ARCH AS IN DIAGRAM Ⓓ

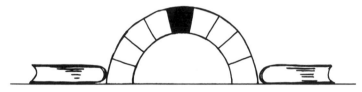

⑤ PUT A 5-GRAM WEIGHT ON TOP OF THE ARCH.

WHAT HAPPENS?

HOW MUCH WEIGHT WILL THE ARCH CARRY BEFORE IT COLLAPSES?

DOES THE ARCH-SHAPE CARRY MORE WEIGHT THAN THE BEAM-SHAPE?

HOW CAN YOU GET RID OF THE HEAVY BOOKS, YET STILL KEEP THE STRENGTH OF THE ARCH?

WHAT KIND OF FORCE IS ACTING ON THE BLOCKS IN THE ARCH? ARE THEY IN 'COMPRESSION' (BEING SQUASHED) OR IN 'TENSION' (BEING PULLED)?

STRENGTH IN SHAPES

YOU WILL NEED:—
3 SHEETS OF BALSA WOOD
2 BLOCKS OF BALSA WOOD.
HACKSAW
HOT-GLUE GUN
PENCIL
5-GRAM WEIGHTS
2 WOODEN BLOCKS

ANOTHER ARCH....

① USE THE WOODEN BLOCKS AND THE BALSA SHEET TO MAKE A BRIDGE AS SHOWN IN DIAGRAM Ⓐ

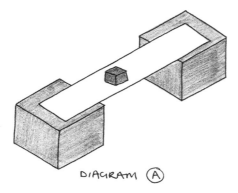

DIAGRAM Ⓐ

② NOW LOAD THE 5-GRAM WEIGHTS ON THE MIDDLE OF THE BRIDGE

HOW MUCH WEIGHT WILL THIS BRIDGE CARRY BEFORE IT SAGS AND TOUCHES THE DESK-TOP ?

③ USING THE BALSA SHEETS AND THE HOT-GLUE GUN, MAKE THE ARCH-SHAPE SHOWN IN DIAGRAM Ⓑ

GLUE THE BALSA-BLOCKS TO THE BASE-BOARD

DON'T GLUE THE ARCHED BALSA SHEET TO THE BASE-BOARD

NOW TEST THE STRENGTH OF THIS ARCH.

PUT A 5-GRAM WEIGHT ON THE TOP OF THE ARCH

WHAT HAPPENS?

ADD MORE WEIGHTS

HOW MUCH WEIGHT WILL THE ARCH SUPPORT BEFORE IT BENDS OUT OF SHAPE?

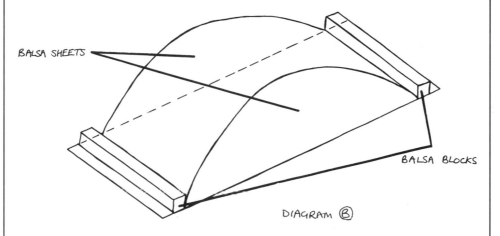

BALSA SHEETS

BALSA BLOCKS

DIAGRAM Ⓑ

WILL THE ARCH CARRY MORE WEIGHT THAN THE FLAT SHEET BEFORE IT BENDS OUT OF SHAPE?

HOW CAN YOU MAKE THE ARCH MORE RIGID?

DOES THIS MAKE IT STRONGER?

WHAT KIND OF FORCE IS ACTING ON THE BALSA WOOD IN THE ARCH?

IS THE WOOD IN 'COMPRESSION' (BEING SQUASHED) OR IS IT IN 'TENSION' (BEING PULLED)?

References

BEASLEY, D. (1984) *Design Presentation*, London, Heinemann.

DEPARTMENT OF EDUCATION AND SCIENCE (1983) *9–13 Middle Schools*, London, HMSO.

ELBAZ, F. (1983) *Teacher Thinking: A Study of Practical Knowledge*, London, Croom Helm.

EM AND YFA (East Midlands and Yorkshire Forum of Advisers in CDT) (1985) *Designing and Making: Learning Through Craft Design and Technology*, Wetherby, EM and YFA.

KIMBELL, R. (1983) *Design Education: the foundation years*, London, Routledge and Kegan Paul.

LIGHT, B. (1988) *Starting Design and Communication*, Harlow, Longman.

SCHOOLS COUNCIL (1974) *Art and Craft Education 8–13*, London, Van Nostrand Reinhold.

TICKLE, L. (1983) 'One Spell of Ten Minutes or Five Spells of Two . . . ? Teacher–Pupil Encounters in Art and Design Education', in Hammersley, M., and Hargreaves, A. (eds) *Curriculum Practice: Some Sociological Case Studies*, Lewes, Falmer Press.

WILLIAMS, P. H. M. (1982) *Teaching Craft Design and Technology 5–13*, London, Croom Helm.

Chapter 5

A Major Breakthrough: The 'Impact' of Design and Technology in a Rural Primary School

Adrian Scargill

The subject now enjoys enhanced status enthusiastically accorded by the Department of Education and Science and H.M. Inspectorate with the accolade of warm approval from Sir Keith Joseph himself. Even in the Primary Schools — once the no-go areas for CDT — the subject is achieving a major breakthrough. (Eggleston, 1984).

Initially the preserve of the secondary school, CDT has, over the last few years, begun to make an impact in the primary school. So how is this breakthrough being manifested?

I shall discuss the experience of the four-teacher rural primary school in which I work, as an illustration of its impact. This will involve reflective views, from the headmistress and myself, of how the subject was introduced and subsequently developed. Through research done in the school I shall describe what I believe is happening in the classroom and relate this to what could be happening, according to perspectives of CDT found in books and published articles. These publications raise the questions: what form should CDT be taking in the primary school? How does this relate to what is happening in my school?

An account by the headmistress, from an interview with her, shows how CDT was introduced into the school. The headmistress initially got involved with the subject about three years earlier, through the use of radio and television programmes in school. Although she could not recollect the programme titles, they dealt with such topics as gears and power. She had started using the television series because of a dissatisfaction with her science teaching. Up until that time, she hadn't really given any thought to CDT and the part it might play in the curriculum.

The work on gears which she then introduced to her own class involved looking at bicycles and how they worked, and using Lego brought in by the headmistress herself. A further programme prompted the idea of making go-karts, and it was through this that a real practical involvement in CDT began. The need to use more durable materials than card and paper was apparent. It was at this point that I first noticed that 'something different' had entered the curriculum. It was difficult not to notice, as full-size go-karts began to spring up everywhere! They were constructed of materials from a variety of sources, using tools brought from home. At that time, the school had no equipment of its own.

ving recognised the value of children solving the design problems involved in building
the headmistress was left with the problem of how to develop and extend that work.
...aving made go-karts, what else should the pupils be doing now that the radio and television
series had finished?

This kind of work, in her view, had much to offer the curriculum of the school, with its
problem-solving approach where the process was more important than the finished product. It
would complement what was already being done in science and environmental and social
studies. The headmistress' role would be to ensure that children acquired the skills necessary to
solve design problems. Because of the work that would be involved, she felt a need to acquire
some of the practical skills required and enrolled on a three-day course organized by the teacher
adviser for CDT. The course was part theory and part practical, introducing a number of ideas
for tasks that the children could be given and then actually making some of them. The interaction on the course with other teachers, some of whom were already doing CDT in their
schools, was invaluable in nurturing the headmistress' interest in the subject.

It was about that time that the same adviser arranged for workbenches to be fitted into
the headmistress' classroom. He also introduced some tools to the school, which were then
added to at some cost, from the capitation allowance: a sign perhaps of her commitment to this
innovation. The staff were then brought together with staff of three other local schools, who
had had similar support from the teacher adviser for CDT, to form a group which would meet
at regular intervals, usually once a term, to discuss the work being done and problems that had
arisen.

At present in the school, second, third and fourth year junior boys and girls take CDT
during the course of a year. This is organized in blocks of six weeks, for one hour a week, so
that each child has at least six hours' CDT per year. A programme of tasks has been thought
out for these three year-groups based upon the acquisition of certain practical skills and increasing demand in terms of problem-solving activity. The headmistress identifies a need to
start a problem-solving approach much earlier in the school and to increase the time spent on it
during the year. She feels that her present CDT group, fourth year juniors, are generally more
capable, both in handling tools and drawing their designs, than were last year's equivalent
group who had no previous experience, and that having a continuous programme can only
improve the eventual quality of work.

The Place of CDT in the Curriculum

The present fourth year group of thirteen children, who I have interviewed and observed, have
been working on a task all term. This task has been to design, make, and evaluate the success
of a mangonel, a medieval ballista. This is one of many other activities involved in a term's
project on the medieval period. The children were initially given a design brief which
presented them with their problem:

'Design a machine that will fire an object at a castle (model). Your machine should have a
fixed arm rotating about an axle. You may choose your own method of propelling the arm
(not your fingers!). Your design must not be longer than 30 cm or wider than 15 cm.'

This brief set limits on the amount of wood that would be used, for cost purposes, and on
the mechanisms involved:

'Your machine should have a fixed arm rotating about an axle.' Otherwise there were few restrictions except that it had to fire an object at a castle. The children were not shown pictures of a mangonel, unless they had difficulty, as it was felt that this would reduce individuality and encourage 'copying'.

The children had to produce a rough drawing of their ideas and, after some discussion with the headmistress about the individual designs' feasibility, a drawing was done on isometric paper to represent three dimensions of the proposal. The aim of the discussion was to ensure that the children were embarking upon something that would work, though possibly with modifications along the way. If a child had produced a design which the headmistress thought would not work he or she was asked to make some form of prototype from card before using wood. This prototype would hopefully highlight the problems and the child could, if necessary, 'return to the drawing board'.

My own initial introduction to CDT happened when go-karts began to take over the school. I noticed the children's obvious enthusiasm for this 'new subject'. I was teaching infants and hadn't felt that my past experience of occasional craft teaching in a middle school had any relevance for them. Shortly afterwards, I changed to a class of second and third year juniors and began to get actively involved by going along to CDT meetings held with the three other schools. There seemed to be some interesting things being made, such as land yachts and cars, and I began to think in terms of what I could do with the children in my class. It was at one of these meetings that the availability of 'kits', for making models such as the land yachts, was first mentioned. These kits contained all the wood and materials already cut to size. Something didn't seem quite right. Was this what we should be doing — making up kits? Nevertheless, I returned to school and, after discussions with the headmistress it was decided to introduce my class to CDT. But what were we going to make? I remembered back to my days in the middle school where I had been given the responsibility for a group making pendants, as part of a system of options operating for the third years. It seemed like a good idea. Although we hadn't got any really suitable wood, it would give the children a gentle introduction to some of the practical skills involved: sawing, filing and sanding. In retrospect, I was at that time concentrating very much on the acquisition of skills and what we could make with those skills. From there, we moved on to making elastic-band-powered boats, an idea I had picked up from one of the meetings. For the first time problems began to arise, and solutions were found. These problems were not only for the children, but for myself as well — how could we best power this boat with an elastic band? If we fix the elastic band there, will it work? Where else could we fix it so that it would be more effective? We were learning together!

After a couple of terms of 'dabbling my toes' the headmistress and I worked out the programme of tasks that could be covered in the top three years. We began on this programme with a group from my class being set the problem of making a vehicle that steered, again an idea picked up from another school. Probably for the first time, in my case, I was setting the children a problem. How were they going to design and make a vehicle that steers?

We began by looking at bicycles, tricycles and model vehicles that steered. How had their designs got over the problem? What methods of steering in the models we looked at could be applicable to the children's designs? This seemed much more satisfying, and motivating; they had problems to solve and no longer was CDT just about the acquisition of skills, though these would become necessary when they began to make the model. It would be then that they would see a need for a particular skill and have to learn it.

The Nature of the Activities

During the course of a few weeks, I interviewed the fourth year children about the work they were doing and observed them making their mangonels. What was at once noticeable was their motivation and sense of purpose. During the lesson I observed, all the children were involved in a variety of tasks, ranging from sawing wood in preparation to build their model, to actually testing its operation and making subsequent alterations to improve performance. The question which occurred to me was:

How realistic was the making of mangonels to the children? Did it seem to them to have some relevance to the rest of their work in school?

The headmistress had seen it as just part of a whole term's project on the Medieval times. The following extract from a taped interview with some of the children was typical of their views and illustrates the relevance in their eyes:

AS [myself]: What's a mangonel, Robert?

Robert H.: It's a thing they used to use in castle times and they had to bash down castles..

AS: Is that the only thing they used to use?

David: A trebuchet.

AS: What's a trebuchet?

David: Something like a catapult.

Kelvyn: (He gives a mumbled explanation)

AS: Why are you making mangonels?

David: We thought they were what the Normans used most.

AS: How did you get into making mangonels? Why mangonels?

David: Because the Normans had them and we're doing about the Normans.

AS: That's what you are doing in your classwork?

All: Yes.

AS: What else are you doing in your classwork about Normans?

Kelvyn: Well, we've been doing about this king and how he lost the Battle of Hastings.

This approach concurs with the view that

> We should not seek to see CDT on the Primary School timetable . . . . CDT activities should be built into the topic area of the Primary school curriculum.
>
> Primary CDT — practical problem-solving — call it what you will — is NOT a subject, but a way of tackling a large part of the primary curriculum, a way of learning which is at once exciting and demanding, questioning and undoubtedly vastly rewarding — for pupils and teacher alike.
>
> The essential practical problem-solving core of CDT philosophy and practice, together with its technological and constructional components, can both infect and affect what happens in primary topic work. (Shaw, 1983).

HMI reported some successful examples of this approach in a middle school where a topic on the Plague and the Fire of London had led to an investigation of tenders, fire engines and pumping devices resulting in the making of fire engines and water pumps (DES, 1980). The lesson I observed was timetabled as CDT as an organizational convenience, so other members of the class (third years) could go elsewhere to do cooking, and it was obvious that the mangonels were not only made on Wednesday afternoon!

Shaw points to the practical problem-solving as the core of CDT. It was this approach that had first attracted the headmistress to it. Was it to be seen in the work the children were doing? How did it manifest itself in the classroom?

In the lesson I observed, most of the children were at some time engaged in finding a solution to a problem, either through the use of craft skills, design or technological aspects of their project. The following extracts from my field notes illustrate the kinds of experiences which pupils were engaged in:

> Penny is working on a mechanism to wind back the arm of the mangonel. She told me that it was her own idea.
>
> Trevor is in the process of putting in some triangular reinforcement. He is doing this because he thought his design would be too weak when he began to fire it.
>
> When Robert H. had completed his winding mechanism he discovered that it was sticking. I spoke with him about it. He saw two ways of getting over the problem — by either greasing the touching parts or enlarging the holes . . . .
>
> Robert has been given another problem by the teacher — to devise some means of holding the mangonel in a ready-to-fire position.
>
> Hannah has not got the two holes, on two sides of the chassis, opposite each other. Consequently, she cannot fit the pieces of dowelling into them.
>
> Simon has put the chassis of the mangonel into the vice incorrectly. When he tries to drill through one of the sides the chassis bends and the joints weaken.

The following taped conversation with another boy (Levi) records how, when explaining his model to me, he realized he had got a problem.

AS: Yours is different to quite a few of the others in that it is flat isn't it? You haven't got those uprights like Trevor's. What made you go for the way you've got it?

Levi: Well, I thought I was going to make it higher, but it didn't seem to go right.

AS: You thought you were going to make it . . . . ?

Levi: Higher up. So that I could sort of hold it back, but I hit that (points) I just now found out and if I stick this on, that will go back and won't fire and it won't ping.

AS: So, how could you get over that problem?

Levi: I'll have to take it off or turn it round . . . . like that. (He demonstrates.)

He continues to demonstrate and explain his solution until

AS: You haven't got the room have you? So you are going to have to do what?

Levi: Raise it higher.

AS: You're going to have to raise that bar up aren't you?

Levi: (Raises bar) Up there.

In these observations, I saw examples of craft (Hannah and Simon), design (Penny, Levi,

Trevor and Robert) and technological (Robert) problems. How should these three elements be reflected in their CDT work? Should one aspect have priority over others or should they be balanced at all times?

Peter Williams defines CDT as being

> concerned with making and doing. It encompasses aesthetic understanding and discrimination (design) and incorporates the acquisition of skills (craft) enabling tools, materials, processes and knowledge to be used in the control of the environment and to satisfy human need (technology). (Williams, 1982).

Williams sees design as the 'unifying factor in CDT' providing a core around which the craft and technological skills can fit. Skills should fit into the designing, problem-solving process as they become necessary. HMI reinforce this point:

> the aim must be to develop skills as they are required during the process of designing and making. (DES, 1977).

The headmistress saw her role as ensuring that children acquired the skills (craft and technology) necessary to solve design problems, the 'design problem' being the 'core' factor. The children were given a design brief initially, which set them their 'problem'.

David describes the 'planning stage':

> David: We had to make a plan and then we had to draw a plan out for a finished design and then Mrs Marett gave us this chart and we had to fill it in — what bits of wood we wanted and then we added it all up at the end to find how much wood we wanted.

After being given the design brief the pupils produced a rough drawing from which they did a 'three-dimensional' drawing and completed a materials chart, which specified exactly how much wood was needed. My observations were centred on the 'making' stage. The project was to culminate by firing at a model castle, 'testing' the model's success.

The headmistress' approach to making mangonels fits into the framework of investigation, invention, implementation and evaluation (APU, 1981). Within it the children were coming across a number of problems. For some children, these problems encompassed all three areas of craft, design and technology. For Penny, Robert H., and some others the task of making a mangonel was providing a design problem through which they were learning new skills and, particularly in the later stages, exploring a technological principle. The extracts from my field notes illustrate that Penny and Robert H. were involved in solving design problems. This also seemed to be the case for a significant number of the children. During the taped interviews quite a number referred to new skills they had had to learn to help them in making their model. For example:

> AS: In doing them, have you had to learn any new skills? Has Mrs Marett had to show you how to use anything in particular, any tools?
>
> Penny: Yes. The drill — I had to put a piece of dowelling in there and drill holes (points to a joint joined by a piece of dowel).

Examples of technology could be seen when Penny and Robert H. were trying to improve both their winding mechanisms and the overall firing performance of the mangonel.

He (Robert H.) has made a slight alteration to his rubber band in order to get a better shot.

Penny is having problems with winding back the mangonel arm. (Field notes).

Process, Product and Pupils' Learning

But what about the balance? There were children for whom the design problems seemed to have become submerged beneath a number of problems relating to their skill proficiency. These children were characterized by having made relatively less progress towards a finished model and they seemed to be faced with a succession of problems for which they did not have the necessary skill. Hannah and Simon were two examples; Rachel was another:

Rachel is struggling with hammering some nails in. (Field notes).

Did the task of making a mangonel provide too difficult a task for the 'less able', in terms of the skills required? How can the headmistress ensure that the children don't get bogged down through having insufficient skills? Lund (1983) suggests that CDT can provide motivation for less able children and that it creates the possibility for improving their self-image and motor co-ordination. But their self-image will only improve if they are able to complete a task and, in the case of these children, complete a mangonel that works. John Lees (1982) suggests a means by which all the pupils can get 'to the starting line at the same time' and successfully produce something that can compete with the others. He sees it as essential that all pupils are able to attempt all sections of the design process. He suggests a system of support to the less able children through which they can be provided with extra resources to stimulate ideas at the planning stage, advice through construction information at the making stage and, if necessary, a detailed stage by stage description of how to construct a basic model. The aim of this support is to ensure that

the ultimate satisfaction, that of finishing a project, is NOT denied them along with any evaluation and development processes which . . . . are an essential part of the design process, as well as being more exciting and motivational . . . . (Lund, 1983).

This desire to finish a project was certainly important in the headmistress' mind, during a subsequent conversation we had, and this had pedagogical implications for her: when, and when not, to intervene in the children's work. There were a number of instances of intervention by the headmistress in the problem-solving process:

He (Robert H.) was working on the winding mechanism. The idea had come from the teacher. The teacher intervened at this point to show him that his holes had been drilled off-square and that this was why the dowel was sticking. She then enlarged the holes for him with a pair of scissors and the mechanism then worked. He was pleased. The headmistress suggested to Penny and Kelvyn that they raise their models off the ground to allow room for a handle to aid winding.

All children mentioned in the taped interviews that they had had discussions with the headmistress after producing the rough drawing of their design. These discussions centred upon the feasibility of the design and, at this point, decisions were made regarding further action.

AS: What did she (the headmistress) talk to you about when she looked at your rough drawing?

Penny: How it would work. How big it would be . . . . the rough size.

AS: Did Mrs Marett talk to each of you about your rough drawing before you drew the three-dimensional one? Or was your 3-D drawing just the same as the rough one?

Kelvyn: She talked to us about what she thought would work or wouldn't work.

AS: Who decided if it wasn't going to work?

David: Mrs Marett.

and later,

David: I had that one as my first design and that didn't work.

AS: Why didn't it work? Did you actually make that?

David: No. Mrs Marett said it wouldn't work. And then I did that one (pointing to another drawing) and that did work.

For David and Kelvyn, the decision about feasibility was taken by the headmistress. Contrast that with the following conversation:

Rachel: . . . . I've done a cardboard one so that it's easier to see.

Penny: Because Mrs Marett didn't think it would work.

AS: So you've made a cardboard one just to see if it would work. I see.

Rachel's design had been quite different to all the others, in fact, it wasn't really a mangonel but more a type of catapult. There had obviously been some confusion initially between a mangonel and a trebuchet and consequently her design was a combination of the two. Despite this confusion, Rachel was convinced that her design would work.

AS: Do you see any problems with what you've got there (a partly made prototype)?

Rachel: No.

and after demonstrating,

AS: Do you see any problem in that at all?

Rachel: No.

Whether or not this conviction persuaded the headmistress to suggest she make a card prototype is difficult to say, but she was certainly treated differently to David and Kelvyn. Was it more difficult to persuade Rachel that her design wouldn't work? Was it right to try to persuade her or was making a prototype the right course of action? Making a prototype would at least enable Rachel to make the decision that it wouldn't work rather than the decision being taken out of her hands. I observed Rachel in the classroom a few weeks later:

Rachel has now abandoned her original design because she didn't think it was going to work. She is now working on something similar to everyone else's though she hasn't committed herself to paper. She says she is going to work it out as she goes along.

I wonder what prompted Rachel to change course? After so many weeks of 'sticking to her guns', she had abandoned her design although her prototype hadn't actually been completed.

Had she 'seen the light' or had she given in to some form of group pressure? Her design was very different to the others and though she is very much an individual, I wonder whether seeing the progress and relative success of the others in the group had had some effect.

There were contrasting forms of intervention. For David and Kelvyn the headmistress made the decision that something was wrong and pointed them in a different direction. For Penny pertinent questions were posed. Rachel was presented with a course of action where hopefully she herself would make a decision. Conversely, I observed situations where there was no intervention, for whatever reason, and because of this problems developed. For example, Robert G. found it difficult to foresee problems:

> Robert G. attached pieces to the end of the rectangular chassis to take the winding mechanism. He is not thinking ahead — he has not thought about how far they should project to allow for the dowel and the string to wind up — it will be very tight as he has not left enough clearance. Penny and Kelvyn have attached stops to the dowel in their winding mechanisms. They have both made the stop too large as it gets in the way when winding up. They are now having to file it down to stop it interfering. (Field notes).

Non intervention in these cases led to the children being faced with a problem which they subsequently solved. Perhaps these problems during the making of the model are not as important as those at the planning stage where significant mistakes could have repercussions for the ultimate completion of the project. They might not make the 'starting line'. The headmistress certainly expressed concern later about whether or not to intervene. Where possible she wanted the children to solve their own problems but she did not want those problems to be so significant that the model could not be completed due to lack of time. She was searching for a balance between the children seeing and solving their own problems and achieving a finished model.

For Future Consideration

In conclusion, I would like to examine the implications of the data, however insubstantial, for the future practice of CDT in the school. Over the last two or three years, the headmistress has moved towards a position not too far removed from that occupied by many writers on the subject. The children in the classroom really did seem to be involved in solving a variety of problems, covering the three elements of CDT and fitting within a framework of Problem-Planning-Making-Testing. One reservation would be that for some children, the less able in terms of skill proficiency, the design problem was lost in an attempt to master too many basic skills. The children were moving from one craft problem to another and as they did so, the concern for the original design seemed to fade.

> It is unlikely that each aspect will develop at the same rate throughout a structured course and to maintain a desired balance, it may be necessary occasionally to separate one for special attention. However, a CDT course will not develop the full potential of pupils if any of these receives little or no consideration. (DES, 1983).

So, for these less able children it mustn't always be craft skills which are concentrated upon. There must, consequently, be careful thought given to the programme of CDT work throughout the school. The headmistress mentioned the feeling she had that this year's fourth years were more skilled than previous groups. To improve this skill level there is a need for design experience to be carefully graded so that, although increasing demands are made upon the children, there are not too many new skills to be learnt during any one task. It may also be necessary, for some children, to give thought to Lees' framework for supporting the less able, so that they are given appropriate help and stimulation before frustration can set in. It is, I feel, important that the children end up with a finished product that works.

Also of help in the design process may be a more extensive use of prototypes, made from card, paper and commercial kits. This would create situations where the children face and try to solve the problems, for some of them do have difficulty in foreseeing them. But this would have implications for the amount of time spent on a project and would certainly need longer than is at present possible.

Finding solutions to problems involves a good deal of appropriate interaction, both pupil–teacher and pupil–pupil. Not only can the child be guided towards solving a problem by asking pertinent questions, but the interaction with peers can also produce possible solutions. The pupil–teacher interactions need careful thought about when to help and how much help is appropriate, and often a conscious effort on behalf of the teacher not to tell them the problem and the solution. Finally, one aspect I would want to change would be to move towards a far more integrated approach where CDT is not just an isolated subject on the timetable. Design problems would have far more relevance coming from either the children's own needs or from other areas of the curriculum, such as science and environmental studies.

References

ASSESSMENT OF PERFORMANCE UNIT (1981) *Understanding Design and Technology*, London, DES.

DEPARTMENT OF EDUCATION AND SCIENCE (1977) *Curriculum 11–16*, London, HMSO.

DEPARTMENT OF EDUCATION AND SCIENCE (1980) *Craft, Design and Technology in Schools — some successful examples*, London, HMSO.

DEPARTMENT OF EDUCATION AND SCIENCE (1983) *CDT: A curriculum statement for the 11–16 + age group*, London, DES.

EGGLESTON, J. (1984) 'Craft, Design and Technology — The uncertain future', *Studies in Design Education, Craft and Technology*, Vol. 18, No. 1.

LEES, J. (1982) 'Mixed ability approach to Technology Projects', *Studies in Design Education, Craft and Technology*, Vol. 16, No. 2.

LUND, D. (1983) 'Craft Design and Technology for Children Having Special Educational Needs' *Studies in Design Education, Craft and Technology*, Vol. 17, No. 1.

SHAW, D.M. (1983) 'Craft, Design and Technology in Primary Schools', *Studies in Design Education, Craft and Technology*, Vol. 17, No. 1.

SHIELD, G. (1982) 'An approach to developing creativity in the field of Craft Design and Technology through small groups', *Studies in Design Education, Craft and Technology*, Vol. 16, No. 1.

WILLIAMS, P.H.M. (1982) *Teaching Craft, Design and Technology Five to Thirteen*, London, Croom Helm.

Chapter 6

Children Solving Problems?

Sally Frost

A colleague and myself presented a 'design and make' task to a group of twelve mixed-ability 10–11-year-old primary school children. The task was to make a toy for a partially sighted child. We attempted to give them equal opportunity to engage in a creative, problem-solving activity that required them to exercise a considerable amount of choice and decision-making. The situation was not entirely new or strange to them. I had taught six of them for two years and five of them for one year. My colleague had taught the same eleven for one year. They were used to working cooperatively on tasks, and had frequently been given the responsibility for organizing, planning and evaluating their own work. The twelfth child, Adam, was from the Area Special Class. The children from this class integrate for several activities with the two seventh year classes. The activity took place on mornings given over to the creative arts when the three teachers and an advisory teacher worked with groups of children on dance/drama, pottery, and a variety of other art/craft activities. Thus the research was carried out within a fairly normal, familiar context with children and staff who knew each other well.

The Teaching Researched

The research was discussed with the colleague with whom I have taught in a cooperative teaching situation, and who shares my views on the intentions of problem-solving. We discussed the educational aim of independent learning and the problems of 'learned dependence'. We both felt that it was important to give all children the opportunity to direct and evaluate their own learning. We were both aware that we at times deliberately imposed what were perhaps false standards of quality, and were interested in seeing what the children themselves would regard as acceptable if left to their own devices. At the same time we wanted to gain some insight into how children of different perceived ability coped with being put into a situation where they were required to work cooperatively, where the teacher acted as guide and adviser rather than instructor.

We chose to work to a set of principles of procedure which were intended to reflect and achieve the aims of independent learning in CDT:

The Teacher's role should be one of guide and manager of the learning situation rather than of instructor and authoritarian figure.

The child's role should be of initiator and active decision maker, who uses the teacher as a resource in his/her learning.

A problem solving/enquiry-based approach should be adopted as being the most appropriate mode of learning.

The emphasis should be placed on the quality of learning process, not the end product or *what* is learned.

Cooperative learning through social interaction with peers is the most appropriate organization of learning.

Active practical activities should be used, and skills should be learned in context rather than in isolation.

Responsibility for the planning, organization and evaluation of the work should be the children's.

Identifying the Issues

I examined the processes involved in the design/problem-solving approach with the group of children, focusing on the following:

The Task

How far did the assigned task allow the child/children scope to make qualitative decisions and act upon them?

The Children

The nature of the judgments made and the opinions expressed at each stage in the process.
The negotiations made in the attempt to find a solution to the problem.
The criteria used to make a final assessment of their own work and that of others.

The Teacher

How did the teacher deliberately or overtly attempt to influence the children's judgments?
How did the teacher deliberately but indirectly attempt to influence them?
How did the teacher unintentionally influence their judgments?
What were the criteria used for final assessment of the children's work?
The teacher's assessment of the children's task performance and her assessment of their ability in design/problem-solving activities.

Methods of Inquiry

These included:

Tape recording of the teacher's introduction to the assignment.

Field notes of observations made during the selection and organization of groups of children, and during the planning stage of their work.

Tape recording to try and record the nature of discussions and negotiations made during the work.

Video recordings of the children working.

Interviews with the children (taped) during work and after the work was complete.

Discussions with the teacher (noted) after completion.

Teacher's post-task perceptions of the activities and performance of different groups recorded in written notes.

Pupils' Responses

The activity was built on assumptions that the conditions created and the strategies used were the most appropriate for the encouragement of independence and creativity, and the promotion of dignity and self-worth. In reality there were different responses to the same experiences. Recent study by psychologists has drawn attention to the *processes* of learning, cognitive style and preferred learning style (e.g. Witkin, 1974; Kogan, 1976). These preferred styles may be acquired through experiences, but may also be part of the child's personality and emotional make-up. Bennett's study (1976) concluded that anxious and nervous children performed better in formal settings, and were less able to cope in informal and unstructured situations, or to take on responsibility for their own learning. When put in such situations, these children would spend little time in positive peer interaction, and a good deal of time wandering aimlessly. Work on 'creativity' and personality, though not conclusive, suggests that creative people tend to be self-sufficient, single-minded, stubborn, persistent, able to tolerate ambiguity and take risks, and capable of a high level of abstract thinking. These studies would seem to indicate that the classroom context and teaching strategies adopted would not suit all children. In the group of twelve children who are the subject of this study, four went some way to meeting an 'ideal pupil' concept, in terms of having some of the qualities necessary to succeed in open-ended, problem-solving situations. They brought these qualities to the learning situation, and subsequent observations and evidence from discussions with the children indicated that they had already become to some extent 'independent' and 'self-reliant', and indeed *wanted* to take responsibility for their own learning.

Simon and Nathan

The two boys were quite articulate about their desire to be given the freedom and right to choose and decide for themselves:

S: I like trying to choose what to do myself and decide I'm gonna do this and work it out myself.

N: I like working by myself, but I get better results sometimes when I'm working with someone else.

They both said that they would welcome the opportunity to plan and carry out their own projects over a period of weeks. They said that they would use the teachers for advice and help (if necessary) and to check written work before presentation. They were critical of some work seen at a recent Schools/Industry exhibition. A group of high school boys (aged about 14–15 years) were making model cars, powered by a pneumatic system. Simon was particularly concerned about the teacher's role in the activity:

S: I don't think they were good enough for boys that age. I think they'd be perfectly capable of making something better than that . . . . I think the teacher may have drawn it on the blackboard and said 'This is your idea . . . . this is how you make it . . . . do it like this and it will come out alright'.

Nathan was more concerned with the uniformity and lack of originality of the finished products. At the same time he shows confidence in his own abilities.

N: I think we could have made them if we'd had all the equipment . . . . and I also think they could have made them a lot better . . . . They were obviously all doing the same thing. They looked almost identical. The teacher had made the mould for them as well.

When asked how they would respond if they were taught like that, Simon replied: 'I would have to go along with it but hope something goes wrong', thus enabling him to take control and solve a *real* problem. Again, Nathan was more concerned with the need to combat uniformity: 'I'd change it a bit'. At the time of the interview, the two boys had almost completed the set task and were now extending it by considering marketing the toy, designing logos, advertising posters etc. I asked them if they felt the task had given them enough scope to develop their own ideas:

SF: . . . . because the task was *set* wasn't it?

S: Yeh . . . . but the rest was left to us. I think it was suggesting use your own ideas — do what you want really.

Nathan said that he likes the sort of task where

N: . . . . the teacher tells you what to do, but you've also got to make up your own mind. Like we're given a task, but we make up our own mind how to do it.

The pair used the teacher for advice about tools and materials and to ask permission to use a display board and space for their presentation. Simon said 'She gave us tips', and this was borne out by observation and by comments made by the teacher. Not only were the boys self-reliant in terms of solving their problem, and competent in terms of applying their practical skills, they were also independent in thought and judgment. They indicated that they thought criticism of work was valuable, but that they didn't accept it if they disagreed. Simon felt that teachers were in an unfair position, because he felt they were allowed to criticise children's work, and usually the child did not have the right of reply. I referred the children back to a situation that had arisen in the previous term, when I had 'implied' criticism of some of Nathan's lettering on a piece of design work. The following exchange took place:

> N: I did some curly sort of lettering and you said 'You're not going to do it like that are you?', and I changed it . . . . because when I looked at it carefully I thought . . . . 'It doesn't quite look right'. When I did it in the first place, I thought that that kind of writing would kind of go with the castle, but it didn't look right . . . . so I changed it.
>
> S: That's the teacher giving *helpful* criticism . . . . Maybe it does sound rude in some cases, but Nathan took advantage of it and sort of worked it out for himself 'No that doesn't look right' and changed it.
>
> SF: I didn't say 'Don't do it'.
>
> S: No. It was alright how you said it 'cause he could have still kept it — you didn't get your way . . . . or . . . . you know . . . .
>
> N: If I'd have liked it, I'd have kept it like that.
>
> SF: I was giving my opinion in a roundabout sort of way.
>
> S: Yeh! 'I don't like that so what you gonna do about it!' (laughs)
>
> N: You probably meant that you thought I could do better if I wanted to.

I asked them when it was justifiable for a teacher to tell them to do something one way or another, or when there were 'right' or 'wrong' answers as opposed to opinions.

> N: There's a wrong way to use a saw, or there's a wrong way to use a knife 'cause you can cut your fingers . . . . Things like that . . . . spelling . . . .

They clearly felt that they do have both the right and the ability to make their own choices and decisions, and to take responsibility for their own work. They planned and discussed their work carefully, foreseeing many difficulties before they arose, and if problems did arise they dealt with them.

> N: From then on things went as planned . . . . we had problems with the wheels as they kept getting stuck, so we took them off and put cotton reels in between, this time they turned, but the wheels slipped, so we put elastic bands on the wheels and it had better grip. (Extract from self-assessment).

Alison and Becky

These two girls also brought qualities of self-reliance to the situations, and demonstrated similar capabilities for independent learning. They liked the sort of task that they had been set, and enjoyed the challenge of inventing things:

> B: I like it when you've sort of been given something to do and design it yourself.
>
> A: I like inventing things. I think it's a waste of time doing something that's already invented.

They rarely consulted the teacher except to ask for materials, or the best way to cut or fix materials. Both of them said that they would like the opportunity to carry out their own project and that the teacher's role within such a project would be:

A: . . . . to help you out . . . . in difficult times . . . . I don't know . . . . I don't
think we would need one. If everyone was sensible we wouldn't need one.

I asked them how they had used the teacher so far:

B: She's . . . . uhm . . . . she's given us advice . . . .
A: She got the ping-pong balls for us . . . .
SF: Have you used her at all?!
A: Yes! We did *speak* to her! (laughs)
SF: So you haven't really needed her?
A: No, not really.

Like Nathan and Simon they too valued other people's opinions, but would in the end judge
for themselves.

These four children were 'ideal' in that they, the task, and the teaching strategies matched.
They were confident in their own abilities, planned work carefully, anticipated possible
problems and showed perseverence when difficulties arose. They accepted the teacher's role as
adviser, but were not dependent on her. They were self-critical, critical of others, but did not
accept criticism unless they felt it was justified. In the post-task evaluation session, their two
toys were considered by the whole group to be the 'best' because they were the most original.
All four children continued developing their ideas further in the weeks after the 'end' of the
research. Because of their success and enjoyment of such activities, they are likely to become
even more confident in their own ability to cope by themselves. If control and ownership of
learning contribute to self-esteem and dignity, these are the sort of children for whom achievement of such aims may be possible within the right setting. However, for the other eight
children, who did not bring the same qualities and abilities to the situation, the experience and
outcomes were quite different.

Adam, Steven and Joanne

Adam and Steven chose to work with Joanne because they said she was 'brainy', 'hard-
working' and 'good at spelling'. Joanne made no decision at all: 'They just came to me and
said we'll work together'. Joanne was nominated the group leader — a responsibility that she
did not want and found difficult to handle. They decided to make a 'walking, barking dog'
based on the ready-made 'walking, miaowing cat' that Joanne had at home. Having drawn an
outline sketch, they found a ready made papier-maché balloon which they were going to use
for the head. They did not address the problems of how to make it walk or bark at all. They
soon abandoned the idea when they could not find a ready-made body to fix the head on to.
They did not approach the teacher for help at all, and when she did initiate discussion with
them, they seemed unwilling or unable to articulate their needs. Adam and Steven spent long
periods of time watching others, staring into space, wandering aimlessly, or fiddling with
pieces of equipment around the room. By the end of week two, the children had found three
buttons and lost one. At the beginning of week three, Joanne came to school with a cut-out
pattern for a rag doll. She asked me if it would be alright to cut out the fabric at school and
take it home to sew up. I said that she would probably have time to cut it out and sew it up
using one of the school's sewing machines, and that I would show her how to use it, but she

was adamant that she would take it home so that her mum could help her. She returned to school the next week with an almost complete, partially clothed rag doll. Only the legs and hair needed sewing on. They attempted to do this in week four with a lot of direction from the Area Special Class teacher. Joanne took the doll home again, and returned with it complete with hair, legs and clothes which her mother had made. She explained that she had to take all the hair out because she had 'done it wrong', and her mother did it for her.

Adam and Steven tried to avoid problems by choosing to work with Joanne, and expecting her to solve their problems for them. They became dependent on her. Comments like 'ask her', 'Joanne decided' and 'it's up to you — you decide Joanne' bear this out. Joanne, faced with this responsibility that she did not want, and with problems that she could not handle, and denied the security of being told what to do by the teacher, solved her dilemma by asking her mother to help her. Her mother reinforced her incompetence and dependence by not *helping* her, but doing the work for her.

When I asked the children at the end of week two what they thought they had learned so far, Joanne replied 'that we're no good'. In the post-task interview, the children all said that they hadn't really enjoyed the work, and would be worried if they were asked to do something similar in the future. When asked how well they thought they had done, Joanne replied:

> Not very well.... we didn't get most of the problems sorted out.... we did something else instead.

Steven still felt that he was 'no good'

> .... because Joanne's done most of the work. Me and Adam done a little bit. Joanne keep taking it home.... I'm not very happy about the way we worked.... because we could all have done all the same if Joanne didn't kept taking it home.

Adam said he hadn't really enjoyed it, and had felt no control over events

> .... because of the way they kept changing their minds what they're doing.... I thought I was in the army being bossed around.... I felt like it.

The children tended to lack confidence in their own abilities. Joanne wrote in her self-assessment:

> When I got into the classroom I was a bit scared of what we were going to do.

Later when asked if she would like to do a project by herself, she replied:

> I'd be worried because I wouldn't be able to do it in time, and.... uhm.... if I didn't get it done I'd have to.... uhm.... catch up with other people.... what they're doing.

Steven and Adam also said that they would be worried, and that they wouldn't have any ideas or know what to do. Fear and anxiety were often related to 'right' and 'wrong' ways of doing things, and a non-acceptance of the teacher's role as guide and adviser was apparent. Again with reference to being asked to carry out their own project the following comments were made:

> J: We need some help really.... because.... uhm.... because you don't really know what to do.

S: I'd rather she showed us what to do.

A: I'd rather be told what to do because sometimes I make mistakes. I could make a mistake with anything.

They saw the teacher's job as helping you 'work'. This work was defined as 'reading, writing, spelling and sums'.

The experience had not enhanced their sense of worth or dignity, but served to reinforce their feeling of worthlessness and helplessness.

Neil and Daniel

Neither Neil nor Daniel enjoyed being left to plan and decide for themselves.

D: I wouldn't like it because as I said before I like to be told what to do.

N: So do I.

Neil was quite clear about what he wanted the teacher to do, but reluctantly accepted that maybe this wasn't what she ought to do.

N: [The teacher's job is] . . . . to think what we're going to do and then teach us. Teachers are supposed to teach you and tell you what to do.

SF: When you come across a problem — what do you want then?

N: An answer . . . . we *need* an answer.

SF: Who from?

N: The teachers, but they don't give us an answer, they help us work it out . . . . I suppose we *should* find out for ourselves . . . .

Both Neil and Daniel seemed to indicate that they knew 'what the game was' but didn't like playing it very much. Both of them said that it was easier being told what to do, and that they preferred it that way. Unlike the 'ideal' children, these children felt insecure in open-ended situations where they were asked to make decisions and choices. To choose and decide involves an element of risk, not only that you may not like your choice, but because things might go 'wrong'.

D: (talking about his glove puppet) I'm a bit worried about how that head is gonna fit in there.

SF: (after some discussion about the problem and possible solutions) You seem a bit afraid of trying out ideas.

D: Yeh! . . . . They might not work and then it gets into a muddle.

This fear of failure was expressed by all five children in one way or another. (Neil said that he'd rather be doing a pencil drawing because he was 'good at that'.) Not liking the risk involved in doing something new was demonstrated by the fact that none of their toys were original ideas, but something done previously, or being done by other groups of children working on different tasks.

Unlike the 'ideal' children, these children usually had a finished product in mind, but did not consider *how* they could make it, did not plan their work very carefully, and did not antici-pate difficulties. Ideas were quickly abandoned if they did not work straight away. Joanne's group decided to make a 'walking, barking dog' because Joanne had a 'walking miaowing cat' at home. A quick outline was drawn in their sketch-book and then they started work. She wrote in her self-assessment:

> We decided to do a dog so we got all of the materials and started to make the dog it was not a success. So we decided to do something else we keep sergesting things then I decided to do a teddy bear with two heads one eye and a punk hair style. So we got to work on the teddy that was not a success because it was too hard so we did not no what to do again . . . . I told Steven and Adam to ask there mums what to do. I was the only one brought a pattern for a rag doll.

In fact, it was Joanne's mother who ended up making the rag doll for her.

The children used a variety of avoidance strategies to evade making decisions or dealing with problems. Because of these avoidance strategies and an over-reliance on others, their skill competence was unlikely to be improved.

Paul

Paul chose to work with Nathan and Simon because he said 'We're normally good at working together see. We normally work well'. Both the teacher and I saw this choice differently. Simon and Nathan are both 'very able', and Paul generally finds practical problem-solving difficult. We both saw Paul's choice as being a deliberate attempt to avoid problems. Subsequent observations and comments made seemed to substantiate this view. The teacher wrote:

> Again Paul has been used to fetch and carry tools, but hasn't really contributed to the project . . . . Paul hasn't been concerned with the design or construction — just with choosing the cotton reels, or fetching the tools needed. He looks to the others to lead. I suppose he has solved his problem! He can't do the task himself, therefore he has put himself with people who can.

In Paul's words:

> I think I'm best at doing the drawing and writing. I think Nathan and Simon are best at, you know . . . . making the actual thing.

When asked how he would feel about doing his own project he replied:

> I . . . . I think I'd have a few problems. I . . . . I like working in groups.

He recognized that he had not really been involved in the problem-solving activity:

> Sometimes they were doing something and I was confused like 'cause I was just standing there and didn't know what I was doing see . . . . so that wasn't for long 'cause then Nathan got me to go and get something . . . . well both of them did, so I got something done.

Evidence gathered from observation, video and field notes backs this up. Physically, Simon and Nathan spent a lot of time working close together, frequently with their backs to Paul, discussing problems, making suggestions, testing and planning further work. They tended to ignore Paul's comments and questions, and often walked away from him when he was still talking to them. They treated him rather like a loved but tiresome puppy that kept yapping at

demanding attention. Paul was very anxious to do something to help them. The
xtracts from field notes are typical of the interaction.

and Simon testing, talking, close together, Paul watching another group
working)

Paul returns: What we gonna do now?

(Nathan explains what they are doing)

Paul:	I'll colour this in right? (label for toy)
Nathan:	We want the writing in blue and the nose red. Right?
Paul:	What's it called then? . . . . Are we gonna put it beside it or what? (No reply from others. Ignored)
Nathan to Simon:	We'll have to mount it.
Simon to Nathan:	Could make it an advertising poster.

(Nathan and Simon discuss advertising. Paul colours Nathan's drawing)

Paul:	What shall I do about this? (no reply) Nathan . . . . Shall I put black round the outside?
Nathan:	Do it like this. Do this first. Right? (Explains and shows Paul how to colour the lettering. Starts it for him)

(Nathan and Simon continue discussing presentation, advertising, etc.)

Paul:	Shall I put the nose red Nathan? (No reply. Nathan and Simon wander off and Paul follows) Nathan . . . . Shall I put the nose red?
Nathan:	Pardon? . . . . Yes. Put the nose red. (Chooses felt-tip pen and starts it for him)

The conversations and activities continue along these lines. Paul asks and carries out explicit instructions. Nathan and Simon discuss, negotiate, test and adapt the toy. In the post-task interview, the group felt that they had succeeded because they had worked well as a group. The allocation of tasks was seen as contributing to this success. Paul did not solve problems, or even attempt to address them, he simply avoided them. Nathan or Simon took on the role of instructor, a role that the teacher had denied Paul. Denied the security of being told what and how by the teacher he has become reliant on other children, who reinforced this dependence by using him as an 'odd-job man', whilst they tackled the real problems of creation and construction of the toy.

Teacher Intervention

The major problem for the teacher(s) became when and how to intervene, so as to help the children, without solving their problems for them. The dilemma was particularly acute with the 'less able' children.

Reflecting on the work done by the different groups, the Area Special Class teacher said that the main difference between the mainstream children and her class, was her children's inability to think for themselves. She said that she didn't feel that she gave them enough opportunity to make decisions for themselves, but decided for them, therefore they never learned to think for themselves. She even 'confessed' to touching up artwork so that it looked better for them to show people. The nature of her intervention with Joanne's group, however, didn't encourage decision-making and independence, but served to exacerbate their difficulties. The teacher spent a lot of time with the group during week four, and the session was videoed. Observations made show how the children were dependent on the teacher to solve their problems for them, and how her intervention compounded their incompetence to perform basic skills.

Adam and Steven were given the task of cutting wool to a given length for the hair, and of trying to sew it on. She showed them how to do this. Steven had difficulty threading a needle. He took it to her and she sent him to fetch a needle with a bigger eye, and then threaded it for him. Later when she had left the room, Steven attempted to thread a needle himself, but rapidly gave up, threw the needle down on the table saying 'Can't do it', and walked away. Joanne threaded it and started sewing on the hair.

Most discussion was directed through the teacher, and the children carried out tasks specified by her. When they finished these they would seek out the teacher to ask if it was alright, and what to do next.

The Area Special Class teacher wrote of the session:

> Neither boy could thread a needle. They set about trying to cut wool and thread hair, constantly asking for assistance, constantly seeking reassurance 'Is this right?' 'I've done this'. If I moved away they would drift out of the classroom to find me. Everything was teacher directed. They couldn't think or try anything out on their own. Adam and Steven couldn't remember what Joanne had done — didn't know that the wool had to be doubled— didn't know how to measure it against one already cut to get the right length. Eventually Joanne threaded the wool and Adam and Steven cut it to length.

The children seemed to have learned to be dependent on the teacher, and unable to operate unless given direct instructions. She reinforced this dependence by telling them what to do and how to do it. She did not help the boys solve their needle-threading problem: she did it for them, and then when they still couldn't do it, she gave the sewing to Joanne to do. She *allowed* them to avoid problems instead of helping them to face them or understand them.

Daniel was trying to make the glove for a glove puppet. He kept drawing onto material and cutting out shapes, with no reference to the size or shape of his hand. The teacher, in an attempt to help him see the problem, kept telling him to draw round his hand and make a paper pattern first:

> If you did it on paper first right? . . . . Cut out a pattern . . . . 'cause you need it for the size . . . . by the time you've sewn round here (cut shape) . . . . your hand isn't going to fit in is it? Get a piece of paper and work out the size you've got to do.

Daniel drew round his hand onto the paper, and cut out the material *without* leaving a seam allowance. The teacher noticed this, but I suggested that she leave him to tack it together. He soon realized for himself that his hand still would not fit in, and then that he needed to allow for the seams. He drew round his hand again, then cut out a larger version, sewed it together, and looked pleased when he could actually get his hand into it. It was not until he got a purchase on the problem that he could devise a strategy to solve it. The teacher's pleas to make a pattern were meaningless until he realized why it was necessary. Teacher intervention in this case created a non-learning situation, which prevented the child from understanding a problem, and devising his own strategies to solve it.

A Curriculum Tension

The educational aim of independent learning through problem-solving seems to require a 'creative' curriculum, and many recent curriculum developments place more responsibility on pupils for decision-making and participation in their own learning. Evidence from this study suggests that some children are better matched than others to such a curriculum. For these children, to some extent well on the way to becoming independent, the task and teaching strategies used resulted in success and enjoyment, and could be seen to enhance their self-worth and dignity. Others, less well matched, seemed to fear failure and tried to avoid taking risks, or making decisions. They devised a variety of avoidance strategies, and their incompetence and dependence was reinforced by their peers, parents and teachers.

My colleague wrote at the end of week two:

> All week I have been asking myself whether we were right to include the 'less able' children in this task. We expect (or I do) that they will not have much success, and they don't appear to have any idea what they want to do. However, the task *is* open-ended, and they *chose* the most difficult thing to do without having any idea of how they were going to do it . . . . They can't organize themselves, and when I question them, they are really waiting (and wanting) me to tell them what to do. If I wasn't aware that this was a piece of research, I think I would have given them a lot more help. Why? Because I don't want them to fail, but as soon as I tell them what to do I am solving their problem for them — thereby compounding their failure. Process not product is the important thing! We have *trained* them *not* to think.

When I discussed this dilemma with the headteacher, he said 'Can't you make sure that they end up with *something* if only for the sake of their self-esteem'.

With the best motives in the world we try to ensure that children avoid confronting failure and dealing with it. Although we claim that it is the processes that are important, our actions suggest that we still either intentionally or unintentionally stress the importance of the product, and this certainly seems to be the message received by some children. Downey and Kelly (1979) claim that coming to terms with your own limitations is part of developing as a person, and that

> For a teacher to prevent a child from attempting something in which he thinks the child will fail is to omit to treat him as an autonomous being or to show him respect as an individual. (p. 25).

This sentiment is reflected in Blyth's 'enabling' curriculum which he proposes should enable choice and acceptance of personal limitations. He criticises primary schools for traditionally creating an unreal world where failure and unpleasantness are 'swept under the carpet' (Blyth, 1984, p. 50). Kanter's (1972) study of the social world of the nursery school reinforces this view of schools. She claims that they limit uncertainty, accountability, and insecurity, and that failure is avoided because it generates 'guilt' which is considered to be psychologically unhealthy. Work on learned helplessness (Seligman, 1975) suggests that a sense of failure is important, and that when failure is avoided or glossed over people continue to go to pieces after experiencing it. When failure is faced and attributed to oneself rather than to uncontrollable external factors, individuals tend to respond more positively and to show improvement in learning. Seligman believes that many failures have developed 'insufficient coping mechanisms' because they have had too much success:

> Their parents and their teachers, out of a misguided sense of kindness, made things much too easy for them.

And further that:

> Unless a young person confronts anxiety, boredom, pain and trouble, and masters them, he will develop an impoverished sense of his own competence. A sense of worth, mastery or self esteem cannot be bestowed, it can only be earned. If it is given away, it ceases to be worth having, and it ceases to contribute to individual dignity. (Seligman, 1975, pp. 158–9).

Joanne, Steven and Adam seem to have learned incompetence and dependence, and are incapable of functioning by themselves, being prepared to wait for others to do things for them. Steven and Adam spent much of the time either inactive or wandering — they seem to have reconciled themselves to being failures and passively accept this. Joanne was anxious to have an end product, her mother produced one for her, but she did not feel any sense of achievement because she had not done any work towards solving her problem.

To deny choice, freedom and responsibility does not value the child as a person. Granting these to children who do not want them, and who cannot or will not handle them, creates anxiety, a sense of failure, and loss of dignity. Clearly the nature of the teacher's intervention is central but problematic. In the case study, when the teacher directly told the children what to do, she stopped them seeing problems and denied them control of their own work. If she just left them to it they floundered, but her attempts to encourage children to see problems and overcome them was sometimes perceived by the children as implied criticism, or an indication that they should not or could not do something: Catch 22!

Paul's willing acceptance of the role of odd-job man gave him security and a sense of contributing to the group's work. Tickle (1983) highlighted the teacher's differential treatment of children. Paul's learning experiences *were* closely controlled and restricted, he *did* continue to work under pressure to perform basic skills, he *was* given jobs that he could copy, and he *was* denied freedom to make major decisions and be creative, not by the teacher, but by his own peers, and through his own preference. The teacher offered him the freedom and right to choose, decide and take responsibility for his own learning, but he did not want it and constantly asked Nathan and Simon what to do and how to do it.

Rowland's research (1982) pointed out how the quality of the pupil–teacher relationship, and the exercise of control over curriculum events, has major implications for the quality of learning experienced by pupils:

> It is not so much the degree to which the students are left to find their own solutions, but the extent to which they exert control over their work, the nature of the teacher's collaboration in this, and the ways in which the student influences the collaboration . . . . When the controlling element on the part of the student is high, his activity is more likely to meet his intellectual needs, and be appropriate to his level of experience. (Rowland, 1982).

Children like Simon, Nathan, Alison and Becky obviously felt a great sense of control over their learning. They wanted this control, and were given the opportunity to exert it. For others, the teacher's intervention denied them control over their own learning because it prevented them getting a purchase on problems. Some children rejected the role of the teacher as guide and adviser, and regarded her as the fount of all knowledge who should tell them what to do. They became dependent on the teacher's help, sought constant reassurance and accepted her opinions and judgments as right. Her questions were not seen as legitimate, but as implied criticism, and an indication that what they had done was wrong. They avoided the risk involved in choosing and deciding for themselves, and by not taking this responsibility, they did not gain a sense of control over their own work.

The tension stems from the main teaching aims. Independence, autonomy and creativity are regarded as worthwhile aims, which can best be achieved through a problem-solving curriculum and teaching strategies which offer children freedom and responsibility, and the right to make decisions and choices. Yet children bring to the learning situation a variety of experiences, personalities and preferred learning styles. Despite the teacher's attempts to treat the children equally, their learning experiences were unequal and to a large extent outside her control. The conclusion that *could* be drawn from the evidence is that because children have preferred learning styles, the teacher *should* perhaps attempt to match her teaching strategies to individual styles. In practical terms this would be difficult, but to instruct and direct children would be contrary to the central aims of CDT, and run counter to the ideal of developing the individual. Further, teacher instruction and direction exacerbates the problem of learned incompetence, and increases the child's dependence on the teacher. I am drawn reluctantly to the same conclusion as Elliott, that you can create the conditions to give children the opportunity to develop, but:

> one cannot make pupils learn autonomously, as one cannot often make them believe or do certain things. (Elliott, 1985).

References

BENNETT, N. (1976) *Teaching Style and Pupil Progress*, London, Open Books.

BLENKIN, G. and KELLY, A.V. (Eds) (1984) *The Primary Curriculum In Action*, London, Harper and Row.

BLYTH, W.A.L. (1984) *Development, Experience and Curriculum in Primary Education*, London, Croom Helm.

DOWNEY, M. and KELLY, A.V. (1979) *Theory and Practice of Education*, London, Harper and Row.

ELLIOTT, J. (1985) *Accountability, Progressive Education and School Based Evaluation*, in Richards (1985) op.cit.

HAMMERSLEY, M. and HARGREAVES, A. (1983) *Curriculum Practice: Sociological Case Studies*, Lewes, Falmer Press.

KANTER, R.M. (1972) 'The Organisation Child. Experience Management In A Nursery School', *Sociology of Education*, Vol. 45, No. 2.

KIMBELL, R. (1982) *Design Education*, London, Routledge and Kegan Paul.

KOGAN, N. (1976) *Cognitive Styles in Infancy and Early Childhood*, New York, Hillsdale-Earlbaum.

OPEN UNIVERSITY, (1971) *Creativity and Learning Styles, Unit 281*, Milton Keynes, Open University Press.

RICHARDS, C. (Ed.) (1982) *New Directions in Primary Education*, Lewes, Falmer Press.

RICHARDS, C. (Ed.) (1985) *The Study of Primary Education: A Source Book*, Lewes, Falmer Press.

ROWLAND, S. (1982) *Progressive Education: A Reformulation from Close Observation of Children*, in Richards, C. (1982) op.cit.

SELIGMAN, M. (1975) *Helplessness*, New York, W.H. Freeman.

SHAW, D.M. and REEVE, J.M. (1978) *Design Education for the Middle Years*, London, Hodder and Stoughton.

TICKLE, L. (1983) 'One Spell of Five Minutes or Five Spells of Two', in Hammersley and Hargreaves (1983).

WITKIN, R. (1974) *The Intelligence of Feeling*, London, Heinemann.

Chapter 7

Promoting Individuality and Originality

Elisabeth Thompson

This report of a six-week investigation into the promotion of individuality and originality in problem-solving skills is related particularly to craft, design and technology. Individuality is taken to be the child's personal way of working and tackling a given problem. Originality is taken to be the use of the child's own ideas, rather than those of the teacher. A main concern which emerges is that of the match between the way an individual child learns and the teaching methods employed to develop the individuality of each child. The focus is on the effect of non-intervention by the teacher (myself) in the learning situation; the hypothesis being that non-intervention would promote greater individuality and originality in solving design problems. The children were given the freedom to make decisions and to be responsible for their own ideas and for the end product, within a series of set problem-solving tasks.

I observed eight children aged 7 and 8 years old tackling six different problems. As their teacher, I tried to keep the contact with the eight children to a minimum, only giving help when help was directly asked for by a child. I noted down places where I would normally intervene, and the places where the children sought some kind of help. I also noted down my idea of what the finished product might be so as to compare it with those produced by the children. Through this device I hoped to discover how much difference there was between an individual adult's conception of the problem and its solution, and the responses of individual children. I suspected that my own imagination in many aesthetic areas of the curriculum influenced and directed the outcome of the children's work and I wanted this to be minimized. Finally the use of skills was observed to see if the child's originality and individuality was restricted by a lack of skills. The implication of this was to judge where and to what extent children need some technical instruction to successfully reach their own solution.

Literature on this aspect of teaching is sparse but the Schools Council book *Children's Growth through Creative Experience* (Schools Council, 1974) was particularly helpful. It discusses the teacher's role and personal patterning of children's working. Ross (1978) also considers the inadequacy of instruction for developing children's personal images. Kimbell (1982) alerts us to the possibility of the development of tool skills and technical competence conflicting with fostering the child's imaginative potential and the acquisition of questioning, exploratory attitudes.

My central concern is the role of the teacher in promoting the best conditions for developing individuality and originality in pupils' work. This may be sub-divided for discussion into issues of non-intervention versus intervention in teaching strategies; the place of technical skills and thinking processes in curriculum content; developing the child's personal vision and ways of working, rather than ensuring conformity; and the importance placed on the end product, compared with the learning process.

Intervention versus Non-intervention

Two broad outlooks oppose each other. Intervention strategists propose that without guidance, instruction and direction the child is severely handicapped in the learning process. Bantock (1968) gives this illuminating example of a teacher using so-called 'free methods':

> 'Make a submarine' the teacher will say indulgently, indicating a chaos of bricks in an apathy of instructional effort. All too often, what these children are doing is thrashing around in a void, unhindered and unhelped by anyone who really knows about the constructional possibilities of bricks and other materials. (Bantock, 1968 p. 78).

Left to themselves children will repeat interminably and often hopelessly the same formalized image or chaotic mess, it is argued. Interventionists say that the further the teacher moves towards allowing freedom of action to the child, the greater the risk that the child will learn nothing at all. In addition, if the child has not had the required training in the technical skills then the inevitable result will be confusion and frustration. In trying to overcome this confusion the teacher may have to help the child so much that she might as well have instructed the child in the first place.

The opposing position of the non-interventionist says that with guidance, direction and instruction the child's originality and individuality and own personal development is stifled by the requirements of the teacher, who imposes her own predigested experience and expectations. Through intervention, uniformity, dependence and acceptance are likely to be nurtured. Children need situations which provide for individual choice and initiative and allow the child to feel a sense of achievement in his or her own efforts:

> Opportunities for children to act upon their environment with their present state of knowledge, even if their actions are neither efficient nor completely understood, are a crucial step in the educational process. The opportunity to explore and investigate the unknown provides support for children's efforts to think independently. They need to take chances, to question why, to see alternative avenues for action. (Brittain, 1979).

Skills and Creativity

Some argue in favour of the teaching of technical skills as a prerequisite so that the child has the competence and confidence to realize a solution. This view often incorporates a belief that skills must be acquired separately, divorced from and preceding any design activity. The opposing position suggests leaving children to think for themselves and to engage in their own exploration of materials in the execution of a design idea, the child having an active role in his or her own learning. Both positions have intrinsic problems. Teaching skills, with the child aiming at an identifiable product, and taught possibly step by step following instructions may mean that

> the pupils carry out the processes without any real understanding and with little personal involvement or contribution. (DES, 1979, p. 3).

Accomplished use of a medium or thorough knowledge of it are not in themselves indications of creative ability. They may be gained through devoted benchwork but the medium may only be wholly mastered in the exercise of creative power, and by the child's effort to shape materials into new configurations. On the other hand, the absence of a skilled technique will mean that a child cannot resolve a problem, and frustration and failure may result.

Idiosyncracy and Conformity

The development of the child's personal ways of working requires a considerable degree of freedom in the learning situation. The child's personal rhythm of work, approach to a problem, and making of a design may only be satisfied through freedom in the learning process. Here, it may be argued, the teacher needs to stand back after providing the materials, to allow the child to tackle a problem in her or his own way, according to her or his own stage of development.

Head Start programmes in Philadelphia came to the conclusion that the classroom structure is an important influence on children's behaviour (Brittain, 1979). They found that highly structured programmes facilitated attention to tasks and conformity to adult expectations. They found such structure less conducive to the development of self-directed and independent efforts to master motor and cognitive skills, or to the application of learned skills in new situations.

Emotionally too the child needs to work out personal ideas. Little emotional satisfaction comes from conforming to the teacher's vision or a sequentially directed formula. In this view, the child's personal vision and preferences will only emerge if he or she is released from conformity.

Product and Process

The issue of the emphasis being placed upon the finished product rather than the process is a recurring one in creative activities. The stereotyped 'model' or the expectation in the teacher's mind may direct the process radically, and determine the product. The emphasis placed upon the end product is part of the strong academic bias in our educational system which makes teachers and parents more concerned with tangible 'results' than with learning which occurs, but which may not be so tangible. An over-emphasis on the finished product can limit the child's imagination to a narrow range of choices and opportunities so that the teacher becomes the 'arbiter and judge, rather than the catalyst and inspirer' (Schools Council, 1974). An over-emphasis on instructional directing, didactically imparting knowledge and skills, may destroy the child's confidence in making anything of his or her own. The thinking may be done by the teacher and not the children. Brittain (1979), studying creativity in a kindergarten, found that it was the teacher who did the planning and came up with the ideas, and the children merely executed commands. Even the so-called creative teacher was imposing ideas and expectations of what the finished product should be like.

King (1978) also points out that what appears to be free and expressive in the classroom is often constrained by the actions of the teachers:

> Creative work is partly organised to reproduce conventional or orthodox reality, a process given greater priority for different reasons when products are to be publicly presented. (King, 1978, p. 35).

When posing a problem the teacher may have fixed in his or her mind (probably unconscious of the effect it is having) a clear picture of the end product and may whittle away at all the deviations children make in their design until their products begin to resemble the teacher's ideas. Mock (1970) comments:

> A teacher who anticipates the result paralyses each child with his own prejudices and imparts false values which are a denial of creative teaching.

Thus my own investigation was motivated by a desire to discover what the role of the teacher should be when dealing with creative and individual aspects of the child. Should there by a definite policy of intervention and instruction to move the child forward into greater skill and knowledge or should there be a definite policy of non-intervention, leaving the child to develop at his or her own rate and to express his or her own individual vision?

The Investigation Conducted

The investigation into the promotion of individuality and originality in problem-solving activities took place over a six-week period with the same eight children between 7 and 8. The role I adopted was that of observer, only giving help to the children when directly asked. Field notes were taken. Observations were specifically directed at the following points:

(a) Moments when, as teacher, I would normally have intervened and my observations of the consequences of non-intervention.
(b) The times when children sought help and why they wanted help.
(c) The way the children tackled the problem, their progress and their evaluation of the end result.
(d) Points where the children needed a skill but did not have it and the result of this.
(e) Points where the children did not see they needed a skill.
(f) Points where the children had acquired the skill but did not see the need to apply that skill.
(g) Before the work started I noted my conception of the end product and compared it with those produced by the children.

The School Context

The school is a large (400 children) primary school situated near Felixstowe. Many parents are employed at the Docks. There are few professional parents, apart from some teachers' children. The parents are interested in their children's progress and support the school in its many activities. Generally the speech patterns of the children are 'restricted', vocabulary is limited and precision is lacking in the children's sentences. The eight children were selected to provide a representative cross-section of sex, ability and personality characteristics. The information is classified in Table 7.1.

Table 7.1

Name	Sex	Ability	Subjective sketch of characteristics
Rachel	F	RA 118. Well above average	Lively, disorganized, slow to settle, imaginative, dreamy, perceptive, intelligent, very careful and neat.
Brian	M	RA 117. Well above average	Quick, energetic, tendency to rush, good all-rounder at work, poor speech pattern, poor motor skills but has intelligent and interesting ideas.
Carole	F	RA 109. Above average	Poor motor skills but a lively and original thinker, good communicator, reasonably good at settling to a task
Keith	M	RA 110. Above average	A very creative, reflective boy, full of ideas, divergent thinker, sensitive, good general knowledge, a leader not a follower.
Angela	F	RA 100. Average	High-spirited, easily led and distracted, lacks ideas, needs confidence boosting, poor at communication, neat, careful worker.
John	M	RA 100. Average	Poor coordination, curious and technically minded, good communicator, imaginative, slow to settle to a task unless interested, dreamy, easily distracted.
Anna	F	RA 95. Below average	Very slow, careful and silent, withdrawn and slightly suspicious. I feel she has untapped strengths but family life stop them from emerging.
Derek	M	RA 92. Below average	Extremely quick and messy, strong personality, interested in all practical work, hates all forms of English particularly reading, very poor speech and limited vocabulary. Good mathematically.

The Learning Observed

The eight children were given six problems over a six-week period. The group was withdrawn from the classroom into the adjoining activity area where materials were provided.

The main research techniques were field notes, observations and interviews with the children.

The six problems were:

1   Design a box. It may be any shape you like and you can make the box from any materials you like.

2   Make a box with a lid and a clasp of some kind so it can be secured. Make the lid fit as tightly as you can.

3   Design and make a simple box or storage tray to keep a collection of sea shells, stamps or rubbers, etc., tidily. The box should display your collection so it is easy to view.

4   Make a container to hold four items found on your teacher's desk — paper clips, drawing pins, pens and ruler. It must be possible to extract the pins and clips easily and the finished holder must look pleasant and be difficult to knock over.

5   Make a piece of apparatus to sort out different sizes of eggs — large, medium and small.

6   Make and design a money box which is fun to use.

No examples were shown to the children during the preparation and execution because I wanted to keep copying to a minimum. The six problems were chosen to produce something within the grasp of a 7-year-old or 8-year-old. Further, there was a skill progression through the tasks.

I have divided the data into two categories. First, there is the record of instances where I would normally have intervened to 'help' a child, but where in these lessons I refrained from doing so. This naturally relies on my own assessment of my own responses, but I tried to be as objective as possible and to note my normal reaction, in each case refraining from intervention. Second, I noted the children's own expressed needs for help, guidance, or materials. In addition, I tried to note each instance of one child beginning to copy another. They could not copy me, or an example, because no 'models' were available to them.

Intervention and Non-intervention

There were distinct and obvious places where I would normally have intervened but I restrained myself because of my wish to act as an observer. These impulses to intervene were recorded and tabulated. A pattern of behaviour emerged. My analysis reveals that the greatest number of 'non-interventions' related to the demonstration of a skill although that varied considerably from child to child. Carole, who has very poor motor skills, topped the list, with Keith and John at the bottom. The sex differences were surprising and not something that I expected to come from this piece of research. Generally the data shows the boys to be more aware of how things are made and dexterous with tools. However the boys also had a tendency to wander away from the design problem. Keith, who I had already perceived as divergent, consistently produced unusual end products which were not always suitable for the objective. For example the series of triangular boxes made in week three for displaying stamps did not match the requirements.

In the section of the observation record 'To show a skill', patterns emerged. There were many instances when I could see a child needed a skill to develop an idea further, for example, how to use a ruler, how to secure sides of upturned paper together, and how to use measuring as an aid to a symmetrical end product. Sometimes the children perceived the need for a skill. For example, in week three all the boys decided to make compartments for their display boxes by using strips of cardboard with slits in and fitting them together. However, none of them perceived that the strips had to be the same size as the length and width of the box and although they cut up equal-length strips they did not fit into the box. 'This is too hard' said John. 'I can't do this'. 'Nor can I' said Keith. Brian came to me quite upset and we talked the difficulties through. This was an obvious moment when intervention would have been beneficial, although I refrained for the purpose of this observation. Usually the children could not see where they needed a technique or skill. For example in week two no child made a satisfactory box with a lid. All of the children devised different methods to try and find a solution. Rachel cut hers on top of the bottom, Keith had two identical pieces of card and carefully measured the folds against the bottom, but some, like Derek, made the two halves independently, so that they did not fit together. Here I feel the exercise was useful because the children were exploring and discovering properties and design problems for themselves. However, because I was anxious not to influence the outcome, I left them at the end with no discussion or instruction. Thus I felt they had experienced the problems but were left floundering. Growth and greater awareness of design would have come from discussion and practical demonstration of how to fix a lid so the sides did not gape.

There was also one instance where the child had the skill but had not perceived the need to use it. This was to do with the ruler which all of them had had instruction with and used regularly in some capacity. I naturally expected in the first week that the children would pick up a ruler, measure the depth of each side and draw a line, but no child in the six-week period did this. Generally the children used 'our eyes' and if one side of the box was higher than the other then they cut it down, judging by eye again, until it approximated the other sides. Some were more sophisticated than others. John used a ruler to make sure the sides of his boxes were level as he turned them up, but he drew no lines; Keith used the ruler for drawing lines and scoring but he did not measure the length; Brian used a ruler to measure and to find the centre point but he then folded the sides up by eye.

Rachel once attempted a measurement. This was in week six when she discovered the sides of her money box were uneven. One was 22 cm and the other 19 cm. I watched her make a 3 cm line on one of the sides which was the place to cut. Then she cut! She didn't measure 3 cm the other side or draw a line across so that the resulting line was uneven. When, in an interview with her later, I asked her why she hadn't drawn a line Rachel said 'I didn't know I had to; no one told me.' When I then asked 'couldn't you have asked me?' she replied 'I didn't know I should have!' This seems an obvious place to step in and show a technique for improving the design. There is no conflict with promoting originality and individuality by leading the children forward into improving their skills. The real problem gradually emerging over the weeks was when should I intervene? Generally it seemed better after some sort of attempt at a solution but not too long after, otherwise they lost interest and this was difficult to recapture. I was beginning to reject non-intervention in favour of a much more complex piece of teaching behaviour related to the responses of individuals.

Problem-posing and Problem-solving

I also monitored occasions when I would normally have given answers or solutions, but where in this work I did not. Some children found a solution independently, as in week one when children decided to use Sellotape instead of glue to join the corners of boxes together. Others could not find solutions to the task immediately, but found a different strategy to re-order the problem. An example occurred in week three where John, Brian and Keith gave up their original design and made small individual boxes to display their rubbers or stamps. Other children became stuck and gave up the task or returned to an earlier stereotype. An example of this happened each week. In week one, Angela could not fit ends onto her rolled cylinder, although she had been taught that technique three weeks earlier. She spent fifteen minutes trying to stick a flat base on to flat edges. Eventually she gave up and left her box without ends. In the third week Angela and Anna did not know how to make a display box; they had not seen one before and had little idea of how to make one. They solved the problem by making the same box as in the previous weeks (large with high sides) to display their rubber collections, without considering the different needs of the problem. Anna made one compartment to separate old and new rubbers and Angela put one isolated piece of card upstanding in the centre of her box. Non-intervention was creating situations of failure for individual children. To focus the children's attention on the design problem, questioning seemed the right approach.

> Judicious questioning serves to orient the child towards phenomena that might otherwise be overlooked or even taken for granted. (Downey and Kelly, 1975, p. 41).

Without some form of discussion vital individual growing points were being lost.

The result of not discussing and questioning was that the children slipped away from the design problem and went off at a tangent. Brian and Derek produced a dispensing till instead of a money box; Anna designed a piece of egg apparatus to make eggs, not to measure them; and four other children in their egg-sorting apparatus forgot a device to sort the eggs. 'Judicious questioning' was certainly needed.

Idiosyncracy and Conformity

The more divergent the worker the more I wanted to keep him or her on target, matching my ideas and stereotype solutions to the task set. Keith and Carole both produced strong responses in me. It is possible that, before this piece of research, Angela's rolled-up paper or Rachel's gaping 'box' would not have emerged from week one. I could feel myself anxious to show them the construction of a box. A notable example of the teacher wishing to direct the outcome was with Carole in week three. Carole had constructed a very large box with high sides. Inside she had made three very uneven compartments from folded card. They were wobbly and stuck in a crooked manner. I could not conceive of this as a display box and asked her twice during its making if this was her intention. At the end we had this conversation:

Observer: Do you like the divisions?
Carole: Yes. They're good.
Observer: But they're not even.
Carole: But I don't want them to be. They're for my stamp book hinges and stamps.
Observer: Won't the stamps get muddled up together? They won't be seen very clearly.
Carole: Well it doesn't matter because they are separate from the other two.
Observer: But don't you want the stamps separate so they can be clearly seen?

Carole:	No. I want to keep them separate from the other two.
Observer:	Are you sure?
Carole:	Yes. It's good.

This is a clear example of the teacher criticizing the child because her end product did not conform to the teacher's vision. Carole's was perfectly acceptable to her. She was 7, had never seen a display box and had not known that individual items were to be kept separate. She had interpreted the problem in her own way.

In the six-week period, because of the lack of intervention, one could see that each child was grappling with the problems at their own level. Possibly because of their efforts and the thought which went into them great pleasure was derived from the finished products although, in my eyes, they were frequently shoddy in appearance. Rachel and John were the only two children who were sometimes slightly unhappy with their results. All the children were pleased with their efforts and persistently asked when they could take them home. The problem was a real one of the teacher, directing outcomes so that the end product matched her own experience of what something should be like but also allowing the children to express their vision at their level of experience.

I also recorded my rather subjective impression of where the children copied each other's ideas. For example, all the children appeared to have copied John's flapped box of week one, although none of the children admitted they had done so. The copying was seldom of a whole idea. Anna and Carole copied Rachel's idea of a slide inside her fun money box; Anna, Derek and Angela copied Keith when he made labels for a container for the teacher's desk, and Derek copied Brian's and John's idea of little boxes inside a large box to display a collection. Occasionally a child would start by copying another child developing an idea but rejected it when they had worked themselves into a difficulty. Brian did this with his egg-sorting apparatus of week five when he copied John's identically. On its collapse he came up with an ingenious and inventive solution. The copying never seemed to be, in the six-week period, damaging to the development of each child's personal expression. An idea was adapted, used or rejected. However, if a child had always copied someone else and never shown any original interpretations then intervention would have been necessary. In Brian's case, copying was an essential step to work himself in to the problem to find a solution. Non-intervention helped him to do this.

Recording children's requests for guidance revealed that in their judgment there was little need for guidance. That conflicts with my perceptions of their needs. However, because of the observation situation, it is difficult to know if this would happen normally.[1] Certainly Brian and Angela perceived me as a reference point and would ask my opinion before they started something or would come to me if they became stuck. Others may have seen a need but were stopped by the situation. From Derek and Keith I gained the impression that they were happy to be left alone to work in their own way and at their own speed. Neither boy ever showed any behaviour which suggested they needed help. Derek quite often came upon design problems but he always managed to resolve them himself. For example in week two he made a lid far too big at each side. Instead of rejecting his design he turned the box over and made the large gaps in each end into a pencil container. However, when questioned later, he mentioned the lid not fitting, implying that he would have preferred a design which did. Again, I feel intervention would have helped. However, the fact that so few children actually sought guidance presents the teacher with the dilemma of intervening when she feels it is necessary and they do not. There is a danger of intervening too early and stifling the child's independence. On the other hand, independent learning by the child can be so lengthy that she or he never reaches a conclusion.

Most of the children's approaches for help were to do with requests for materials. 'Can I have some sponge', or 'Can I have some Sellotape' were typical questions. Requests for help with handling materials were for cutting thick card or securing things together with unsuitable adhesives and it might be fair to say that from this six-week research project the children saw me as a provider and manipulator of materials and not as a consultant or instructor.

Standing back and observing provided a picture of individual pupils' modes of working. Derek rushed into a problem and then found he had not thought it out carefully enough. Angela did not concentrate on the problem, worried about not being able to do it, fiddled and then had problems finishing in time. Anna rarely talked to anyone, nor asked for help or externalized her thoughts. Rachel and John were quick to see solutions and to start but got sidetracked into inessential details. Keith liked to do his own thing and did not like interruptions, while Brian liked discussing the problem and watching others.

Conclusion

A very clear conclusion was drawn from this six-week study. Non-intervention did not promote originality and individuality. It allowed the children freedom to work in their own way at their own pace. Yet they were caught in their own lack of experience and skills. The children were enabled to realize the problems for themselves but without instruction did not move forward to solutions. They could adapt an idea, turn a failure into something else, but their ability to solve technical problems and develop ideas seemed very limited indeed. Although the children had been at school for over two years, not one of the eight used a ruler correctly in a six-week period! What seems to the adult to be a simple technique (matching the top and bottom of a box together) did not emerge from any of the children. I am therefore in no doubt that 'judicious questioning' or direct intervention would have vastly accelerated the move toward solutions and improved their learning.

However, the study also produced clear evidence that the children were absorbed in their work and were very proud of their products. Their motivation was good, so that they were ready to be stimulated and guided. The problem facing the teacher is how to stimulate and guide without imposing too many preconceptions and stereotypes, and without stifling the child's own creative and logical thinking and making.

My reactions to the problems being solved and those of the children showed no correspondence at all. Thus some of the art of teaching would seem to lie in giving the children the right problems to develop particular skills, whilst also judging what is meaningful to them. The problem must allow the child to discover a skill and challenge his or her thinking process but should not be too 'total' a problem so that the child is overwhelmed and discouraged. 'Luminous familiar spots from which helpful suggestions may spring' (Kimbell, 1982) are essential for the child to 'gain a purchase' on the problem.

The process of interaction noted in this study is complex. What seems to a teacher to be the right time for intervening may not be the right time for the child; the teacher is always working with the need to make judgments. Those judgments are difficult because the creative process is 'essentially subjective and private and mysterious, requiring unconscious as well as conscious action' (Ross, 1978). The teacher has the problem of whether, when and how to become involved in such action. The children in this study were content to 'do their own thing' with a minimal amount of intervention so the role emerging for the onlooker was that of an interested adult, giving help and support and only intervening when the child seemed hesitant about either his or her own skill or the next direction to take in the construction.

Notes

1. The children gave innumerable signs of being conscious of the scribbling away as seen through furtive glances after I asked them questions and wrote something down. On five separate occasions when I moved away from my notes different children tried to read them; Angela and John asked me what I was writing and Derek asked what I was going to do with the notes. Thus I feel the children may have been unusually inhibited in seeking help from me.

References

BANTOCK, G.H. (1968) *Culture, Industrialisation and Education*, London, Routledge and Kegan Paul.

BRITTAIN, W.L. (1979) *Creativity, Art and the Young Child*, London: Collier.

DEPARTMENT OF EDUCATION AND SCIENCE (1979) *Curriculum 11–16*, London, HMSO.

DOWNEY, M.E. and KELLY, A.V. (1975) *Theory and Practice of Education*, London: Harper and Row.

HUDSON, L. (1967) *Contrary Imaginations*, Harmondsworth, Penguin.

KIMBELL, R. (1982) *Design Education: The Foundation Years*, London, Routledge and Kegan Paul.

KING, R. (1978) *All Things Bright and Beautiful*, Chichester, John Wiley and Sons.

MOCK, R. (1970) *Education and The Imagination*, London, Chatto and Windus.

ROSS, M. (1978) *The Creative Arts*, London, Heinemann.

SCHOOLS COUNCIL (1974) *Children's Growth through Creative Experience*, London, Van Nostrand Reinhold.

WILLIAMS, P. (1985) *Teaching Craft, Design and Technology 5–13*, London, Croom Helm.

Chapter 8

Children and Choice: Making Decisions in Design

Alan Rosenberg

HMI, the DES and others have called, over the years, for a greater degree of choice, opportunities to take initiative, and the use of problem-solving in our schools (Board of Education, 1931; Central Advisory Council, 1967; DES, 1985a). They have also sought to promote cooperative learning:

> In all the schools the children responded favourably to opportunities for cooperation when these were offered . . . . Very few of the schools were good at providing opportunities for children to exercise choice or initiative but about half provided some, more often for older pupils than younger ones. Children displayed initiative more often in the context of craft subjects than elsewhere. (DES, 1985a, paras 3.4. and 3.6).

Notions such as practical learning, learning through doing, and a reaction against didactic pedagogies are implicit in the 'practical' subjects of art, design, craft, and technology. It is in the arts that problem-solving is sometimes found in our schools (Gulbenkian Foundation, 1982; Tickle, 1983, 1987). A style and pedagogy of emancipation and liberation from rigidly controlled learning is implied here: education is to empower the child, it is to confer dignity upon the adult by accepting the dignity of the child. The child is not seen as Rousseau's 'flower to be watered' but as an integral part of society with individual needs viewed in a social context. Hargreaves' (1982) notions of dignity and community development reflect this view of schooling. Gone the behaviourist's rats and other quadrupeds — instead we are offered children who learn to explore, expand and express by being allowed so to do. Part of this liberating process is learning to make decisions by making them, learning to cope by coping and learning to cooperate by cooperating in the same way that Bruner (1960, 1971) suggests that we learn and become physicists by doing physics, mathematicians by doing mathematics, and so on.

It was in the spirit of education as a liberating, dignifying and humanizing process that this small piece of fieldwork was undertaken at Heartsease First School, Norwich. A design activity was chosen for observation because it held the promise or revealing aspects of cooperation, initiative and decision-making by the children.

The activity researched was the making of a frieze by a group of infants. I wanted to act both as teacher (enabler) and researcher: to facilitate success but to step back as far as possible

114

from the decision-making process. I aimed to observe how the children chose the subject; selected the materials; cooperated, conflicted or competed with each other. I also wanted to see how tasks within the joint endeavour were chosen or allocated; how great an area of choice children use with a minimum of teacher intervention; and how they perceived the success or otherwise of the activity. A further concern was to consider the nature of the role of the teacher as a group member rather than as a group leader, and to see how children valued the work of other members.

The Group (top infants aged 7)

I discussed the objectives with the class teacher, and worked with six children of *her* choice for two mornings (a Friday and the following Monday). She chose the group as being of perceived mixed ability. The children all knew each other well and me not at all. I was, therefore, in a situation in which they had to teach me a lot about the school building, the administrative arrangements and, of course, about themselves.

There were three girls: Tracy, Gemma and Stephanie; and three boys: Jason (Blond), Jason (Brown) and Matthew. I tried to adopt the roles of an enabler, a teacher/researcher, and a group member — identifying with the success of the task, but making a conscious effort not to impose ideas and solutions; not to dominate.

The Task

Choosing the subject of a frieze, the materials to be used, discussing various stages, constructing and evaluating the product. It was perceived as an exercise in designing, as a cooperative group enterprise.

The Situation

A light, airy school which, due to falling rolls, had some empty rooms. One such room served as a craft room in which a very wide variety of art and craft materials were kept. A welfare assistant did small group work in this room. Children could thus be sent there for materials and receive help. The group was allocated a room in which we could work undisturbed for two mornings.

Research Methods

(a) A discussion of what I would like us to try and do:
   who I am, why I'm there and an introduction to the group.
(b) Audio tape of discussion focused on selecting the subject of the frieze.
(c) Audio tape of children undertaking the activity.
(d) Field notes, where possible given my dual role as observer and participant.
(e) A post-task interview with the children.

A Picture of Events

The sample of data concerning how the children chose the subject is illuminating (after establishing names and a chat about who I am and why I'm there, a fifteen-minute introduction in which I met Stephanie, Gemma, Tracy, Jason Brown, Jason Blond and Matthew):

AR:	I want to see how we can make a picture working together and talking about it as we go along. Gemma, what would you like to do?
Gemma:	A summer picture.
AR:	Fine, fine. How do you think you'd set about it? What would you need to do a good summer picture? (7 secs) Now all of you listen because you're all going to be asked what you would need to do what you want. It may be that we haven't got what you need. Can you, in your head, see a summer picture? Have you got an idea of a summer picture?
Gemma:	(6 secs) Flowers. (7 secs) Grass. (20 secs)
AR:	Keep thinking about that OK and I'm going to come back to you. Tracy?
Tracy:	A winter time picture.
AR:	You fancy a winter picture. What do you need to do a winter picture?
Tracy:	Leaves. (8 secs) Trees.
AR:	What colour are the leaves?
Tracy:	Brown.
AR:	No houses? (to Gemma) No houses in your picture either?
Gemma:	No.
Tracy:	No.
AR:	You don't want houses?
Tracy:	No.
AR:	Fine. (to Tracy) (20 secs) — No hurry, we've got all morning. Do you want me to come back to you? To leave you thinking about that and I'll go on?
Tracy:	Yes please.
AR:	Could you say your name again please. I'm bad with names.
Stephanie:	Stephanie.
AR:	What would you like to do Stephanie?
Stephanie:	A jungle (There was a picture of two tigers on the wall in front of her).
AR:	What do you think you'd need to do a jungle? To do a good jungle.
Stephanie:	Tigers.
AR:	What do you think a jungle looks like? What colours is it mainly? (15 secs) I mean if I said to you 'Right, we'll do a jungle, go and mix me some paints.' What colour paints would you use? (15 secs) Have you ever seen a jungle Stephanie? (21 secs) On television?
Stephanie:	Yes.
AR:	What colours? It's full of plants. What colours are they — mainly?
Stephanie:	Green.

AR: All different kinds of green, that's right. And what colour are the trunks of trees?

Stephanie: Brown.

Gemma offered a summer picture and was then encouraged to investigate how she would set about it and what it might contain. It was a brilliantly sunlit winter day. Her response was slow, hesitant and thoughtful: 'Flowers . . . . Grass.' Could the articulation of those two words really have occupied thirty-three seconds? No — this is a young girl faced with a total stranger to whom she is trying to give an 'acceptable response'. She, however, has nothing upon which to assess the likely reaction of her questioner. She may be striving for the right answer — trying to please the teacher.

Tracy suggested a winter picture. Neither of the girls wanted houses. Stephanie's 'jungle' may have been prompted by a striking picture of two tigers in a jungle setting, on the wall in front of her. Even then her single-word answer was coaxed from her. I used ninety words, Stephanie used six. You can almost hear me struggling on the tapes. Whatever was happening to her?

All the boys wanted to do space. 'Now there's a good answer' I said. Space was partly legitimized. Matthew's responses was positive and constructive. Only Jason Brown — described by his teacher as 'very slow' — recognized the divergence of response and provided a synthesis in the form of a workable compromise.

Jason Blond: (clowning slightly) Mm . . . . Mm . . . . Mm . . . . — Space.

AR: What do you know about space?

Jason Blond: That there's loads of spaceships and loads of stars.

AR: What do you think you'd need to do a really good space picture.

Jason Blond: Black paper?

AR: Black paper. That could be arranged. Jason Brown — and you?

Jason Brown: Space.

AR: Why do you think you want to do space? (17 secs) Is it because he said it first? (16 secs) You haven't got an answer to that question have you — you haven't really thought it through?

Jason Brown: It's interesting.

AR: Now there's a good answer. Matthew?

Matthew: I'd like to do space and put in all the planets and the moon.

AR: Have you done one before? Have you done a space picture before?

Matthew: I've done a small one at home.

Stephanie: It's a big bit of paper.

Jason Brown: We could do space at the top and a summer picture at the bottom.

AR: I'm going to leave you for five minutes and when I come back you tell me what you want to do.

(AR leaves)

Reading the first pages of transcript of this group's choice-making it becomes apparent that the children were not as free as I had hoped (and supposed) they were. Firstly — I had decided that the activity would be frieze-making. Secondly — the size of the frieze was determined by the paper available. Thirdly — the children had in no way volunteered, they had been selected as 'a balanced group'. They had not chosen the activity — or each other. Fourthly — of forty-six contributions Gemma made three, Tracy made six, Stephanie made seven, Jason Blond made three, Jason Brown made three and Matthew two. I made twenty-two, several of which were quite long. The teacher (non-interventionist you will recall) wins the word count hands down. The score was 'combined children' 80, teacher 330.

The attempt to get children to think in words about their preference — and my not wishing to favour one of the four options and to remain *neutral* actually resulted in me not sanctioning or legitimizing any of them.

Reading the transcripts carefully, it seems that the children had been sent to do something *for me* and had been making suggestions for me to accept or reject. Some of the teacher responses were less than encouraging — though they don't sound too bad on tape. For instance 'Why do you think you want to do space, is it because he said it first?' (16-second pause) You haven't got an answer to that, have you?' Far from being a happy cooperative little band, we were at this stage a teacher-dominated and manipulated group in which everybody's choice had been rejected by somebody and none of them had been accepted and legitimized by the teacher. When I left the room the purpose was to remove the dominating and inhibiting presence BUT — the guidelines were laid down: 'I don't mind what we do at all. But we do have to agree about what is done.' — 'I'm going to leave you for five minutes and when I come back you tell me what you want to do.'

In the next minutes the pattern of response changed. Jason Brown made ten contributions, Jason Blond eighteen, Matthew twelve, Stephanie four, Gemma ten, and Tracy fourteen. The most evident person on the tape at all times is Jason Blond.

New ideas were introduced in an attempt to do something for the teacher, who remained the task-setter and legitimator: 'If you don't want to, we'll tell the man'. There is a dire threat of redundancy in Jason Brown's 'He might choose some more children'.

Castles and battles appear, Superman, something really good, tigers, lions, a farm, Jason Blond's persistent space — and Stephanie's jungle:

Jason Blond:	(Enthusiastically) Space.
Chorus:	No, No.
Matthew:	Why should we do what you want?
Tracy:	Do the sea.
Gemma:	We could do the sea.
Matthew:	Alright let's.
Tracy:	We could do the sea.
Chorus:	of Nos with one Yes.
Jason Brown:	We've got stuff for the sea.
Jason Blond:	The water.
Matthew:	Yeah.
Jason Blond:	Steph's the only one who don't want to.
Chorus:	Yeah.
Gemma:	We could do fishes and that.
Tracy:	What about a boat?
Matthew:	A lot of fishes and sharks.
Jason Blond:	Loads of submarines.
Tracy:	We'll do the sea.
(Jason Blond starts making wave noises)	
Matthew:	We'll do the sea.
Gemma:	We'll do the sea.

Tracy:	(referring to Stephanie and Jason Brown)
	If you don't want to we'll tell the man then.
Matthew:	Who votes on doing the space?
Chorus:	(giggles)
Matthew:	Who votes on doing the sea?
Jason Blond:	Who votes on doing the castle?
Matthew:	Who votes on doing the jungle? Who votes on doing the sea again
Two Voices:	No. No.
Matthew:	When the man gets back we'll do the vote, shall we?

Jason Brown ('very slow') made intelligent and constructive contributions which display a practical attitude to the decision-making and a grasp of the politics of the situation:

'It's interesting'
'A castle'
'Why can't we mix in the two together'
'We've *got to do* things'
'We've got stuff for the sea'.

Then, when he thinks he's going to lose his castle — 'I don't want to do the sea'.

Matthew's attempt to bring order to this by calling a vote (to invoke and utilize a social procedure which would lend authority to and legitimate a decision) was stymied by Jason Blond taking over and by Tracy's response ('Why should I tell you?'). The sea emerges as an accommodating idea which can include islands, a castle, fish, the sky — but space is lost. The final decision is made very quickly when the teacher returns to the room. There is, in this event, some genuine coming together of the group — albeit to please 'the man'. There are conciliation strategies — the vote, the sea, mixing the two together. There is derisive banter: 'You could do the castles — that's rubbish'; and defiance: 'Why should I tell you?'

The teacher has, however, set them a task — presented them with a problem and demanded a solution, which he will then ratify or not. They have fulfilled their task — done what was expected of them and solved the problem — for the teacher.

The paradox of a liberal pedagogy, enabling choice, initiative, discovery, etc., in a hierarchical social structure which contradicts most of its principles is revealed in Bowles and Gintis (1975):

> The most progressive of progressive educators have shared the common commitment of maintaining ultimate top down control over the child's activities. Indeed much of the educational experimentation of the past century can be viewed as attempting to broaden the discretion and deepen the involvement of the child, while maintaining hierarchical control over the ultimate processes and outcomes of the educational encounter. The goal has been to enhance student motivation while withholding effective participation in the setting of priorities. (Bowles and Gintis, 1975, p. 39).

With regard to the selection of materials: the children chose and used a wide range and seemed to be prepared to use anything available. They used transparent plastic, metalized paper, frieze paper, wallpaper, paint, brushes, sponges, felt, egg-boxes, wool, tissue paper, a shoe box, the pressed plastic from chocolate boxes, etc. Frequently a child faced difficulty with adhesives or cutting and my help was constantly sought — but never about the content of the frieze —

always about how to do something. Jason Brown for instance was perplexed and frustrated by water-based paints refusing to 'take to' a polystyrene egg-box.

Throughout the task the group seemed to work as individuals: Matthew on the sky, and a Camembert cheese-box sun; Stephanie on her jungle and a vast number of tiny, golden fish; Jason Brown on his castle; Gemma on an island; Jason Blond on fish and boats and divers; Tracy on some trees. It would have been interesting to discover whether this was a type of territorialism, or a sophisticated strategy for cooperating by avoiding competition. Was it a continuation of the individual task tradition — each child painting their own picture? Although the children were supportive of each other, kind, and showed each other their contributions for comment, I was surprised at the frequency with which my assistance was sought to solve problems and to permit: 'Sir, is red allowed?'. The odd border incident or boundary dispute was settled without rancour. This work supports Kirby's observation that

> The younger the children the more frequent will be the return to the centre; to the teacher for reassurance, encouragement, guidance and further teaching. (Kirby, 1981).

The children were very appreciative of each other's contributions — indeed three hours of tape recording contain no child's criticism of another child's work despite the fact that conversation about the ideas and techniques was incessant. Although children concentrated on separate task areas their communication was collaborative:

Jason Brown:	Here we are — there's a boat. We can use some of this for a stick.
Jason Blond and Tracy:	Yeah.
Tracy:	I'll cut it and stick it like this so it looks as if it's filled up with wind.
Jason Brown:	Is this alright?
AR:	Put it on and have a look.
Jason Blond:	Yeah. Cut that through.
Jason Brown:	Is this big enough now, this sail?
	Is this big enough now, this sail?
Gemma:	You could do the sails.
Jason Brown:	Yeah — I could do two sails. I could do two sails.

Five people are involved in this decision.

When we had finished, the children were very pleased with the frieze but they could all think of things they would do to it had they more time. They all thought it was better than they expected. They all said that I gave them enough help and they all appreciated that the workload was shared. The question 'What do you think is the worst thing about it?' brought no response at all. Jason Blond, Tracy and Stephanie thought the work 'beautiful', Gemma 'attractive', Matthew 'excellent' and Jason Brown 'colourful'.

The activity, on reflection, does not illustrate that children left alone will create and learn to do so by a 'sort of apprenticeship'. It does, however, indicate that given time and patience children will cooperate in problem-solving and enjoy that cooperation.

References

BOARD OF EDUCATION (1931) *Report of the Consultative Committee on The Primary School* (Hadow Report), London, HMSO.

BOWLES, S., and GINTIS, H. (1975) *Schooling in Capitalist America*, London, Routledge and Kegan Paul.

BRUNER, J.S. (1960) *The Process of Education*, Cambridge, Mass., Harvard University Press.

BRUNER, J.S. (1971) *The Relevance of Education*, London, Allen and Unwin.

CENTRAL ADVISORY COUNCIL FOR EDUCATION (1967) *Children and Their Primary Schools* (Plowden Report), London, HMSO.

DEPARTMENT OF EDUCATION AND SCIENCE (1980) *A Framework for the School Curriculum*, London, HMSO.

DEPARTMENT OF EDUCATION AND SCIENCE (1985a) *Education 8-12 in Combined and Middle Schools*, London, HMSO.

DEPARTMENT OF EDUCATION AND SCIENCE (1985b) *Better Schools*, London, HMSO.

GULBENKIAN FOUNDATION (1982) *The Arts in Schools*, London, Calouste Gulbenkian Foundation.

HARGREAVES, D. (1982) *The Challenge for The Comprehensive School*, London, Routledge and Kegan Paul.

KIRBY, N. (1981) *Personal Values in Primary Education*, London, Harper and Row.

TICKLE, L. (1983) 'One Spell of Ten Minutes or Five Spells of Two? . . . . Teacher–Pupil Encounters in Art and Design Education', in Hammersley, M., and Hargreaves, A. (Eds), *Curriculum Practice: Some Sociological Case Studies*, Lewes, Falmer Press.

TICKLE, L. (Ed.) (1987) *The Arts in Schools: Some Research Studies*, London, Croom Helm.

Technology 5 to 11

Proposals of the Science Subject Working Group of the National Curriculum Council.

Outline

5.1   This Chapter presents our recommendations for the technology curriculum 5 to 11 in detail. It sets out the four attainment targets we recommend for the 5 to 7 key stage and the 7 to 11 key stage, together with the relevant parts of the Programme of Study which are associated with those attainment targets. Also associated with each attainment target are the statements of attainment which set out what each pupil will be expected to know, understand and do in order to have reached that level. The corresponding TGAT levels are placed on the right of the statements of attainment in the spread sheets. The four attainment targets for each key stage are grouped into one profile component.

5.2   As with Science we have used certain terms in our statements of attainment concerning knowledge and understanding. The meanings we attach to these terms are repeated below:

'Know that' means that recall is expected.

'Know about' means that a generalised awareness of a subject is expected, without necessarily having detailed recall. This more generalised knowledge can be focused through different contexts.

'Understand' means that a pupil is able to apply and use knowledge in new, given situations.

5.3   But before turning to our recommendations for Technology in detail we believe it may be useful to explain our understanding of Technology and its place in the primary curriculum because it is only recently that it has begun to become established.

Technology in primary schools

5.4 Some aspects of Technology have always been present in primary schools, mainly in practical activities in Science, Mathematics and Craft. As teachers have developed a way of working through themes and topics, which is unrestricted by subject boundaries, they have often introduced aspects of Technology in problem solving, without necessarily using the term, or understanding the whole process. Some teachers are helping children undertake worthwhile practical activities which are not technological; others concentrate on one aspect of Technology only, whilst a growing number are undertaking a range of technological activities, sharing their ideas and expertise with others.

5.5 This curriculum area is growing and developing in primary schools, but as yet there is no wide agreement among teachers as to what it should constitute in terms of primary practice. Despite several valuable national and local initiatives, it will still be some time before it settles into its place in primary schools as a whole, and we recognise the need for research and development in this area over the next few years.

5.6 Our views on Technology 5 to 11 are based on the good practice now developing in some schools. They take into account that there are many primary classes where this work has yet to begin with primary children, and others where able teachers, with and without appropriate resources, are helping their children to achieve very high standards.

5.7 In describing our framework we have tried to strike a balance between using the language of technology and using terms which will be more readily understood, so that those unfamiliar with technological language will not be deterred. As teachers and children work in this area and begin to gain familiarity with the language and processes of technology, they should grow in confidence and generate a mutual enthusiasm, helping to build up good primary practice in the future.

5.8 Much of children's early technological experience comes from solving problems and responding to the needs created by their imaginative play. They may need to cross a stream, build a den, climb a wall or sail a boat. To do this they need to arrange and order things around them to create desired structures. They will use materials which are to hand and begin to find out about them, choosing them to suit a purpose, fixing them, modifying them. They will learn about these structures, how to make them stable, and by the process of trial and error, seek to control or improve their world. These activities provide a range of experiences which can be harnessed and developed by the teacher within the classroom.

5.9 At the primary stage, children learn about the world around them mainly through first-hand experience and with the help of teachers develop important skills, concepts and attitudes. They do not see the boundaries between one form of knowledge and another. Since Technology draws from many areas of the curriculum and uses the knowledge and understanding it needs from them to solve problems, it fits quite appropriately into the primary classroom.
Thus:

- children making a series of houses to defy the efforts of the wolf to blow them down will need to know something about materials used for building and ways of fixing them to make strong structures;

- children building a Norman castle will need to know something about the Normans' way of life and the problems of that period in history to help them understand why the Normans built castles as they did and used the methods they did. This will help the children make realistic models;

- after watching a parachute drop, a group of children could develop their own parachute, and explore, for example, different materials and canopy design;

- through Geography, children will begin to see how people use and adapt their environment and build effective homes or shelters using local materials. They will find out how people move around, transport their goods and materials, and how they trade;

- through Physical Education they will be involved in activities of balancing, bending and twisting; they will begin to feel the forces involved, and relate these to work in other areas;

- through Mathematics, they will learn about some of the two- and three-dimensional shapes they are using, how precision of measurement of length and angle matters, and the importance of scale.

5.10 As problems are identified and solutions sought, children will be able to draw from a wide range of experiences, of which some will have been guided by the teacher, some will have been shared with others and some drawn from other sources such as televison.

What is Technology?

5.11 From the wide range of valuable activities in primary classrooms, it is useful to draw out some of the features which characterise technological activity:

- it is concerned with practical problem-solving to meet a purpose or respond to a need;

- it is concerned with designing and making;

- it draws on a wide variety of experiences, knowledge and skills from many subject areas;

- it involves the need to investigate, innovate, make and evaluate;

- it can involve designing a system and putting it into effect;

- it is concerned with open-ended problems which are capable of having more than one solution;

- it is concerned with optimum rather than correct solutions, and allows children to express their own views and preferences.

5.12 Since Technology involves practical solutions to problems, it is mainly associated with the knowledge and skills of Craft and Design, Economics, Mathematics and Science.

From **Craft and Design** it draws on knowledge of:

- materials and the way they can be worked;
- tools, and methods of use and safety;
- aesthetic factors (including effects of colour, pattern and texture);
- the ability to communicate design ideas.

From **Economics** it draws on ideas which become very important at a later stage:

- consideration of availability of materials;
- consideration of the cost of the materials and the process used and the time taken;
- consideration of the value of the project in view of the compromises which have to be made.

From **Mathematics** it draws on:

- knowledge and understanding of shapes — both two- and three-dimensional;
- spatial awareness;
- the need and ability to estimate, computate and measure;
- the ability to use scale.

From **Science** it draws mainly on:

- skills of exploration and investigation;
- materials and their properties;
- forces and structures;
- energy and the way it is controlled;
- knowledge and understanding, including living things, which can provide the context of much technological activity.

Technology and Science

5.13 Technology and Science are closely linked and many teachers have come to Technology through activities they regard as practical Science. There are however distinct differences. Because Science is enquiry-led and discovery is for its own sake; the conclusions are drawn from the evidence and data and are as objective as possible. Technology, on the other hand, essentially involves meeting a need or solving a problem. The best solution will often involve a subjective judgement, and will be arrived at after taking a wide range of factors into account.

5.14 A summary of Technology which may be helpful is:

'Technology involves a creative human activity which brings about desired changes by making things, controlling things or making things work better by careful designing and making, using relevant knowledge and resources.'

Processes Supporting Technological Activities

5.15 Technology is not the only way of solving a practical problem; the solution is technological if it involves designing and making something.

5.16 In this process children need to understand

the needs of others

eg before you design and make something to improve a blind person's life, you need to know about the problems of blindness;

or before you decide to attract birds to build nests in your garden, you need to know about the habitat and behaviour of the birds you wish to attract; and

the use of structure and materials

eg before you design and make a device to lift and move a heavy object, you need to understand that when materials are assembled in a particular way they are capable of lifting and moving heavy loads. Moreover there are alternatives. Some may design a system which involves the use of lever and rollers, some a block and tackle and others may design a crane.

5.17 As children develop their technological capabilities, they need to develop their awareness, capability and understanding, all of which are closely inter-related.

5.18 Children should be given the opportunity to study the results of Technology and the solutions which other people have found to problems. They should see how human ingenuity and innovation have resulted in some surprising solutions to problems. They should have the opportunity to observe how each generation or group has improved that solution, refining it in the light of changing need. Thus:

- before designing and building a tunnel under the Channel, however great the need, you should realise that it will have strong implications for the whole social structure and ecology of the local environment, patterns of transport, jobs, and many other issues which will need to be considered.

Children need to learn to develop their judgements on the results of Technology, both on its benefits and its drawbacks.

5.19 Children will begin to understand that there are a number of approaches to solving problems. Whichever approach is used it is expected that the process will show evidence of:

(i) Observation, investigation and enquiry

These will arise naturally as children explore the context of their problem, decide what needs to be done and what conditions need to be met. A sharing of such findings with others helps to broaden the understanding and widen the range of solutions that could be explored; children may in this way learn to modify their ideas.

(ii) Recording

Children should be encouraged to record the outcomes of their observations as a first step towards developing a solution. This may involve drawing or writing, or the use of other media such as tape recordings or photographs. Such records help children form hypotheses and promote imaginative and inventive solutions to their problems. Discussion of this material with others again plays an important role.

(iii) Designing

From their recorded observations children explore possible solutions to their problem and, as these ideas clarify, so they are considered, discussed, refined or rejected until one is selected for development. They then decide how and with what it will be made. This is the beginning of technological design and it can be a short or long process.

(iv) Making

From the preliminary design stage children plan how they will interpret their designs into three-dimensional forms. During this 'making' process their design may need to be modified or others added. At this stage the children aim to produce models or artefacts which attempt to find a solution to the original problem, but in doing so they come to recognise how aesthetic considerations of quality and appearance affect their solution.

(v) Evaluating

Children should evaluate the outcome to see if it satisfies the original intention.

The Results of Technological Activities

5.20 The work which children undertake in Technology will be broad and varied. They may result in, for example,

- a dragon made from scrap material which roars and which has flashing eyes;
- a model crane like the one they saw on a visit to the docks;
- a device to feed the goldfish whilst children are away on holiday.

On the way to achieving their solution, the children may have experience of:

- investigating ways of making a switch;
- designing a pulley system;
- investigating the control, timing and methods of delivering food.

5.21 Technological solutions have to 'work', ie satisfy the original problem, and one way to assess the outcome therefore is to encourage children to ask themselves

- does the solution work?
- does it solve the problem?
- have I accomplished what I set out to do?
- could I make it work better?
- have I used the most appropriate materials?
- is it aesthetically pleasing?
- have I considered such factors as cost and time taken?
- why does it work?
- what helped me when designing it?
- how did I overcome any difficult parts of the design?

5.22 As children gain in experience so they will refine their thinking and develop their making skills. They will be able to tackle more complex problems and produce solutions which show a developing awareness of aesthetic qualities, manipulative and communicating skills. They will begin to develop a deeper understanding of the world, their culture and how it developed. This should give them experience and confidence to handle uncertainty and make them feel able to tackle and solve today's problems and live in tomorrow's world.

The Framework for our Recommendation

5.23 From this background we have drawn four essential strands:

- Technology in context
- Designing and Making
- Using Forces and Energy
- Communicating Technology

Each of these plays an important part in the whole process. They will not, however, always be present in the same proportion all the time by the very nature of the diversity of the problems being tackeld and the capability of children involved. But we recommend them as the four attainment targets which make up the one Profile Component, Technology 5 to 11. Details are set out in the spread sheets which follow.

Technology in context

Attainment Target 1

Children should know that the response to the needs of the living and man-made world has often resulted in a technological solution. They should understand that there can be benefits and drawbacks, and realise that this has implications for their own lives, that of the community and the way we make decisions.

Relevant part of the Programme of Study

5 to 7 Children should be given the opportunity to develop an awareness and understanding of the needs of the living and man-made world (for example, food, water, shelter, transport and medical care) through a range of everyday, personal and imaginative contexts, and recognise the advantages and disadvantages of different solutions.

7 to 11 Children should develop a growing awareness and understanding of technological solutions to problems both in historical and modern contexts. This can be done through a range of themes, topics, visits or everyday situations giving children the opportunity to study solutions such as:

- a range of solutions from everyday products to major engineering works such as castles, bridges, canals or docks;

- those involved in growing plants for food or pleasure, keeping animals at home, school, on farms or in zoos;

- technological systems involved in manufacturing common foods, (for example, bread, dairy products) and how they are prepared for consumption;

- systems for controlling traffic flow, moving products or people;

- successful solutions to similar problems, such as things that fly, dig, move on land, in air or through water, support tall structures, cut tough material;

- technology in the context of disease and its potential to reduce the effects of physical disability.

They should be encouraged to appreciate that the solution to one problem may result in causing another.

Statements of Attainment

Children should

LEVEL

- know that a problem can have more than one solution.   **1**
- be able to identify a need which requires a simple technological solution.

- be able to suggest solutions which show that they are aware of advantages and dis-   **2**
  advantages proposed.

- know how the basic needs of life (food, water, transport, communication) have been   **3**
  solved by people, animals and plants.

- be able to distinguish similarities and differences within a group of successful solutions   **4**
  to similar problems (man-made and natural).
- be able to give reasons for the choice of design and the materials used when considering technological solutions, products or systems.

- be able to appraise products or systems from an industrial, agricultural or commercial   **5**
  setting.

Designing and Making

Attainment target 2

Children should be able to design and make an artefact, product or system. They should be able to select and use materials to match specific needs; be able to use tools safely to cut, join and mould them with due regard to aesthetic and functional properties.

Relevant part of the Programme of Study

5 to 7 They should be given the opportunity to experience a wide range of designing and making activities, using a variety of materials. They should be involved in investigating, planning, designing, making, modifying and evaluating with appropriate guidance. They should develop or acquire further knowledge and skills when needed.

They should have the opportunity to handle a wide range of everyday materials, both natural and man-made, investigating similarities and differences whilst exploring their physical and aesthetic properties.

They should have the opportunity to work with them in a variety of situations – folding, bending, twisting, cutting, joining and altering the surface (painting or sticking things on it).

7 to 11 Children should be given the opportunity to experience a wider range of designing and making activities through which they can develop a growing technological capability. They should experience and show evidence of identifying tasks which require a technological solution; observing, collecting information or data, and investigating that which they consider useful; putting forward solutions, selecting and modifying where necessary, taking account of constraints; making their final solution. They should test it and evaluate it and be able to communicate what they have done in an appropriate form.

They should have the opportunity to handle a wider range of natural and man-made materials, both flexible and rigid, and tools to work them (shape, hold, cut, join). They should use these materials to build structures, working models or other artefacts which give pleasure and/or satisfaction when tackling a specific problem.

They should be encouraged to relate the physical properties of the materials to the uses to which they may be put.

They should have the opportunity to experience the designing and implementing of a system such as a production line, taking account of economic factors, for example, cost and time.

Statements of Attainment

LEVEL

Children should:

– be able to design and make simple artefacts related to the context of the classroom or   **1**
their lives.

– be able to choose the most suitable materials from a given range and give reasons for
their choice.

– be able to handle simple tools carefully and safely, (for example, scissors), when
cutting and joining easily worked materials into desired shapes.

– be able to solve a problem by designing and making an artefact in a context relevant to
their lives.

– be able to modify their design or make adjustment where necessary.   **2**

– be able to select from a range of everyday materials those which are most appropriate
for what they intend to do or the visual effect they want to achieve.

– be able to use hand tools safely, to cut and join appropriate everyday materials; use
simple adhesives.

– be able to investigate the context of the task and extend their knowledge where   **3**
necessary.

– be able to select and use pliable and rigid materials appropriately when building structures, working models or artefacts.

– be able to use a range of hand tools safely, with some degree of accuracy and concern for the finish achieved.

– show that they have considered the appearance as well as the working efficiency of their artefact when evaluating their solution.

– be able to select and use a range of materials to build a variety of standing and moving   **4**
structures.

– be able to measure and cut a range of materials with some accuracy.

– be able to recognise the need for relevant background information and be able to apply it.

– be able to observe, identify, investigate and collect information or data which is useful.

– be able to recognise deterioration caused by constant use or environmental factors and suggest simple ways to prevent it, (for example, treating the surface).

– be able to test and evaluate their solution against their original needs.

– be able to design and make an artefact which shows an increasing quality in the   **5**
finished product which should be aesthetically pleasing as well as functionally sound.

– be able to suggest modifications which might improve the overall effect achieved.

– be able to identify and select appropriate materials for a specific task.

– be able to use protective finishes in an aesthetic way.

– be able to use a wider range of hand tools safely, to fashion materials using techniques of construction.

Using forces and energy

Attainment Target 3

Children should be able to develop and use their knowledge and understanding of forces – both static (in structures) and dynamic (in moving things). They should develop and use their knowledge and understanding of energy, its sources, uses and ways of controlling it.

Relevant part of the Programme of Study

5 to 7 Children should be given the opportunity to create structures and engage in activities which enable them to experience pull, push, twist and balance.

They should be involved in constructional activities which enable them to make things move and stop them moving; explore a variety of mechanisms including toys and equipment; and use simple devices such as wheels and rollers.

They should play with and investigate familiar objects (including toys) where energy is stored, controlled and released; gain insight into the forces resulting from using water, weights, sand, wind and themselves as energy sources.

7 to 11 Children should be involved in a range of practical activities which help them to experience and take account of forces such as tension, compression, torsion, bending, friction and gravity.

They should experience a wider range of energy sources including magnetic and electrical.
They should be given the opportunity to explore and use levers, cranks, gears and pulleys.
They should experience the possibilities of the inclined plane, hydraulic, pneumatic, magnetic and electrical devices.

Their work should also include the use of information technology for storing, processing information and controlling energy (such as moving a buggy-vehicle or working a lighting system).

Statements of Attainment

Children should be able to:

	LEVEL
– use forces to push, pull and twist in order to move devices.	1
– build a variety of structures from everyday materials.	
– construct something and make it move.	
– make structures which show they have taken into account simple forces to pull, push, twist, bend and balance.	2
– recognise two energy sources and use one of them to make a device move	
– take into account where friction needs to be increased to provide grip or reduced to make things move more easily.	3
– modify a structure to take account of increasing forces acting on it.	
– select from a variety of energy sources and use it to make a device move.	
– control the energy flow using simple devices.	
– use triangulation to make a structure more rigid.	4

– use devices such as gears and pulleys to achieve movement at a desired speed.

– use a range of energy sources knowing when they are appropriate.

– use electrical, magnetic and mechanical methods to control the flow of energy.

– use a computer to store, process or control information.

– make structures showing they have considered the size, shape and material from   **5** which they have made it to withstand forces.

– select and use a mechanism from a variety of alternatives to change direction or speed of movement within a device.

– select and use appropriate energy sources and control them using mechanical, hydraulic, pneumatic or electrical devices (including computer control).

Communicating Technology

Attainment Target 4

Children should be able to communicate clearly their stages of thinking, designing and making and evaluating using a variety of means such as modelling, drawing, oral or written, mathematical or computer techniques. They should be able to select the most appropriate method for the audience or purpose.

Relevant part of the Programme of Study

5 to 7 Children should be given the opportunity when designing and making to develop and use a variety of communication skills and techniques (talking, listening, discussing, writing, drawing or modelling).

These activities should allow them to become familiar with more precise technical terms, using them to tell others what they have done and what they are going to do, with reasons for their choices.

They should have opportunities for asking questions, seeking answers, discussing and evaluating their ideas with their teacher and other pupils.

7 to 11 They should develop an increasing competence to talk and write about their activities, what they found out, observed, investigated or made, representing their ideas through drawings and diagrams where appropriate. They should develop the ability to translate two-dimensional drawings or plans into three-dimensional shapes.

They should be encouraged increasingly to select the form of communication most suitable for the material to be communicated and the audience who will receive it.

They should experience the use of a computer for word processing, and data handling.

They should have the opportunity to use a computer to monitor aspects of change in the environment (such as temperature or animal behaviour).

Statements of Attainment

Children should be able to:

LEVEL

– talk about what they have done.   **1**

– represent what they have done by a combination of drawing and modelling.

– explain what they have done in sequence.   **2**

– use drawings and notes where appropriate to help communicate the thinking behind their final artefact.

– communicate, using appropriate vocabulary, what they have done and their thinking,   **3** planning and making. They should give reasons for any modifications.

– take part in discussions about a design problem, generating and sharing ideas.

– use a simple data base to store, retrieve and use information for designing.

– communicate in an appropriate way the process by which they arrived at the final   **4** artefact.

– discuss the planning and ideas which were rejected as well as accepted.

– show how they may have redesigned or remade parts.

– use IT techniques to help when designing.

– receive and exploit ideas from a variety of sources.   **5**

– communicate ideas for the solution of problems using appropriate vocabulary, graphical techniques, flow diagrams, and two- or three-dimensional modelling.

– use a computer to monitor information about change in the environment.

Design and Technology: Key Stages 1 and 2

Proposals of the Design and Technology Working Group of the National Curriculum Council.

For key stages 1 and 2 (5–7 and 7–11 years) the final report of the design and technology working group recommended that the range of levels of attainment which should apply to pupils at the end of each key stage should be levels 1–3 and 2–5 respectively, following the system laid down by TGAT. Separate programmes of study were provided for each level, and each programme related to all four attainment targets. The programmes are in two parts, the first describing 'the nature of the activities which enable design and technological capability to be developed' and the second 'what should be taught'. That is consistent with the approach of the interim report, which set out to reflect the holistic nature of the processes of design and technology, and described the knowledge and skills as a 'resource-base' to be used in the activity.

Attainment Target 1

Identifying Needs and Opportunities

Through exploration and investigation of a range of contexts (home, school, recreation, community, business and industry) pupils should be able to identify and state clearly needs and opportunities for design and technological activities.

Attainment Target 2

Generating a Design Proposal

Pupils should be able to produce a realistic, appropriate and achievable design by generating, exploring and developing design and technological ideas and by refining and detailing the design proposal they have chosen.

Attainment Target 3

Planning and Making

Working to a plan derived from their previously developed design, pupils should be able to identify, manage and use appropriate resources, including both knowledge and processes, in order to make an artefact, system or environment.

Attainment Target 4

Appraising

Pupils should be able to develop, communicate and act constructively upon an appraisal of the processes, outcomes and effects of their own design and technological activities as well as of the outcomes and effects of the design and technological activities of others, including those from other times and cultures.

Statements of Attainment and Programmes of Study for Levels 1–5

Statements of Attainment – Level 1

AT 1 Describe to others what they have observed in familiar contexts (*for example classroom, home*) or visualised about imaginary contexts (*for example a desert island, a lunar landscape*).

Suggest what might be done in that context (*for example make a model, organise something in a different way*).

AT 2 Represent their ideas about what they might do (*for example by modelling materials, role play*).

AT 3 Use a variety of materials and components, tools and equipment to make simple models, drawings and structures.

AT 4 Describe to others what they have done and how satisfactory they think it is.

Describe to others what they like and dislike about familiar artefacts, systems or environments.

Programme of Study for Level 1

At Level 1 Pupils Should Develop Design and Technological Capability through Activities:

● which each involve all the attainment targets, and which are always purposefully developed in response to perceived needs or opportunities;

● based on contexts which are within their experience, both imaginary and realistic, *such as children's pictures, poems and stories, the home, the school and local shops;*

● some short and some extended, arising from a variety of contexts;

● which involve role play and visitors, *for example parents and other teachers;*

● undertaken individually and in groups which develop personal qualities necessary for successful design and technological work.

To Achieve Level 1 Across the Attainment Targets Pupils Should be Taught:

Materials and Components
● to handle, use and explore a variety of materials and components *such as fabrics, paper, card, 'dough-like' materials, disposable products and construction kits.* (Also applying aspects of Science AT 6.)

Energy
● to use purposefully sources of energy, *such as elastic bands, moving water and falling weights*, in making things move and change.
(Also applying aspects of Science ATs 10 and 13.)

Business and Economics
● to recognise that goods and services are bought and sold.

Tools and Equipment
● to recognise, handle and use safely a variety of simple tools.

Aesthetics
● to recognise in their work and surroundings aesthetic characteristics of line, shape, form, structure, colour, pattern and texture.
(Also applying aspects of Mathematics ATs 10 and 11.)

Systems
● that a system or an environment is made from a number of related parts which combine to achieve a particular purpose, *for example observing clocks, bicycles, or play shops, play houses.*
(Also applying aspects of Science ATs 10, 12 and 13.)

Structures
● to recognise the simple structures around them and use components to make some themselves, *for example making towers or buildings from simple construction kits.*

Mechanisms
● to recognise that materials and components can be linked in

various ways to make movement, *for example exploring toys and everyday articles like hinges and zips.*
(Also applying aspects of Science ATs 10, 11 and 13.)

Exploring and Investigating
● to observe and talk about a variety of familiar products.
(Also applying aspects of Science ATs 1 and 12, Mathematics ATs 1, 9, 12 and 13 and English AT 1.)

Imaging and Generating
● to use their imagination in creative activities, *such as story telling, role play, drawing, painting and modelling.*

Modelling and Communicating
● to represent their ideas, *for example by talking, role play, drawing, painting and modelling.*
(Also applying aspects of Mathematics ATs 12 and 13 and English AT 1.)

Organising and Planning
● to plan a simple sequence of activities, *such as sorting and matching, jigsaws and pattern making.*

Making
● to use a variety of materials and tools to make simple models, structures and environments.

Appraising
● to talk about what they have done;
to talk about why they like and dislike things, *such as places, clothes and pictures.*

Health and Safety
● that any tools and equipment they use should be used correctly and safely.
(Also applying aspects of Science AT 11.)

Social and Environmental
● to talk about the needs of people, animals and plants.

Statements of Attainment – Level 2

AT 1 Ask questions which assist them to identify needs and opportunities for design and technological activities in familiar contexts (*for example about how something works, how things are done*).

Describe what they have observed or visualised and found out in their exploration of familiar contexts.

Suggest some purposeful and practical changes that could be brought about (*for example of colour, form, function, organisation*).

Describe to others why they made the choices that they did.

AT 2 Represent their ideas about what they might do (*for example by making models, role play*).

Use pictures, drawings, models, to develop their design proposal, giving simple reasons why they have chosen a certain idea for making.

AT 3 Use their knowledge of the working characteristics of materials (*for example will it take glue? will it tear?*) and components, including construction kits, in making artefacts, systems or environments (*for example models including ones which work and move*).

Use a variety of simple hand tools and equipment safely.

Demonstrate when making that they can use materials and components appropriately.

Describe to others how they are going about their work.

AT 4 Discuss with teachers and others how satisfactory are the results of their design and technological activities, including function and form, bearing in mind their original intention and how they went about their task.

Make some simple value judgements about familiar artefacts, systems or environments, including those from other times and cultures (*for example how well it works, how pleasing is the appearance*).

Programme of Study for Level 2

At Level 2 Pupils Should Develop Design and Technological Capability Through Activities:

- which each involve all the attainment targets, and which are always purposefully developed in response to perceived needs or opportunities;

- based on contexts which are within their experience, both imaginary and realistic, *such as children's pictures, poems and stories, the home, the school and local shops*;

- some short and some extended, arising from a variety of contexts and requiring increasing breadth of knowledge, skills and values;

- which involve simulations, role play and visitors, *for example parents, other teachers*;

- which provide opportunities to look at the artefacts, systems or environments created by others;

- undertaken individually and in groups which develop personal qualities necessary for successful design and technological work.

To Achieve Level 2 Across the Attainment Targets Pupils Should be Taught:

Materials and Components
- to handle, use and explore a variety of materials, media and components; *such as fabrics, paper, card, 'dough-like' materials, disposable products and construction kits;*
- the properties including weight, strength and texture;
- the working characteristics of materials and components, *for example capable of being joined, mixed and formed.* (Also applying aspects of Science ATs 6 and 11.)

Energy
- to use purposefully sources of energy, *such as elastic bands, batteries, moving water and falling weights*, in making things move and change. (Also applying aspects of Science ATs 10 and 13.)

Business and Economics
- that goods and services are designed and made, distributed, bought and sold.

Tools and Equipment
- to recognise, handle and use safely a variety of simple tools and equipment when designing and making;
- how simple tools function and how to look after them.

Aesthetics
- to make choices about the use of aesthetic characteristics in their drawings, paintings and modelling. (Also applying aspects of Mathematics ATs 10 and 11.)

Systems
- that a system or an environment is made from a number of related parts which combine to achieve a particular purpose;
- that control is making things do what they want them to do, *for example steering, lighting, switching.* (Also applying aspects of science ATs 10, 12 and 13.)

Structures
- to explore materials and components to make simple structures for a purpose, *such as containers and fantasy beasts.* (Also applying aspects of Science AT 10.)

Mechanisms
- to explore and use materials and components, to make simple things that move, *for example rubber bands, cotton reels, paper clips and lollipop sticks.* (Also applying aspects of Science ATs 1 and 12.)

Exploring and Investigating
- to ask people about their needs;
- to gather, organise, store and present information when designing and making. (Also applying aspects of Science ATs 1 and 12, Mathematics ATs 1, 9, 12 and 13, English AT 1 and Information Technology AT.)

Imaging and Generating	● to visualise and recall experiences as a stimulus for their creative activities *such as talking, role play, drawing, painting and modelling.*
Modelling and Communicating	● to represent and develop their ideas by drawings, models and language;
	● to use role play to enact their own and other people's experiences and needs. (Also applying aspects of Mathematics ATs 12 and 13 and English ATs 1 and 3.)
Organising and Planning	● to plan a simple sequence of activities, *such as sorting and matching, jigsaws and pattern making.*
Making	● to select and use appropriate materials, tools and equipment for their making activities.
Appraising	● to talk about what they have done, what they have learnt and what they might do differently next time;
	● to make a simple appraisal of products, *for example toys, buildings and clothes* and ask questions, *such as: Why was it made? What was it made of? How is it put together? How does it work?*
Health and Safety	● that any tools and equipment they use should be used correctly and safely;
	● to care for the environment in which they work. (Also applying aspects of Science AT 11.)
Social and Environmental	● that resources are not infinite and that some technological solutions can cause damage;
	● to recognise that people like and need different things.

Statements of Attainment – Level 3

AT 1 Investigate familiar contexts in a number of ways including finding information from relevant sources (*for example books, databases, people*).

Use scientific, design and technological and other knowledge (*for example of people, materials, production and distribution of everyday products*) to assist their investigation of contexts and their identification of needs and opportunities for design and technological activities.

Review their emerging ideas about possible needs and opportunities for design and technological activities with those involved and use this review in identifying these more clearly.

AT 2 Record, using appropriate media and methods, their explorations of different ideas about design and technological proposals to see how realistic they might be.

Use information about materials, people, markets and processes from their immediate environment (*for example shops, schools, homes*) and also from other times and cultures to help in developing their ideas.

Form a design proposal by selecting from their ideas, giving reasons for their choices (*for example of function, style, use of resources*).

Apply knowledge (*for example of equipment and materials they have used*) and skills (*for example from their own work and the work of others*) in order to select ways of realising the different parts of their design.

Use drawings and modelling (*for example annotated drawings, sketches, working models, simple measurement*) to develop their design proposals.

AT 3 Use their knowledge of the working characteristics (*for example is it easy to shape? will it float?*) of natural and manufactured materials and components to choose appropriate resources for making.

Use a given range of hand tools and equipment, appropriate to the materials and components involved, safely and with some regard for accuracy and quality when making.

Take account of constraints of time and availability of resources in planning and making.

Improvise within the limits of their materials, resources and skills when faced with unforeseen difficulties.

AT 4 Discuss with teachers and others the results of their design and technological activities, taking into account, where appropriate, how well it meets the needs of others.

Comment on the materials and processes used and how they went about their tasks.

Programme of Study for Level 3

At Level 3 Pupils Should Develop Design and Technological Capability Through Activities:

- which each involve all the attainment targets, and which are always purposefully developed in response to perceived needs or opportunities;

- which are developed progressively to extend their experience from contexts which are familiar, to ones which are less familiar;

- some short and some extended, from a variety of contexts and requiring an increasing breadth of knowledge, skills and values;

- which offer some opportunities for them to identify their own tasks for designing and making from within given contexts;

- which involve simulations, role play and visits or visitors, *for example local businesses or service industries*;

- which provide opportunities to look at the artefacts, systems or environments created by others;

- undertaken individually and in groups which develop personal qualities necessary for successful design and technological work.

To Achieve Level 3 Across the Attainment Targets Pupils Should be Taught:

Materials and Components

- to identify common natural and manufactured materials;

- to join common materials and components in simple ways;

- to use materials, media and components that are appropriate for the task in hand, when designing and making;

- to recognise that materials can be worked in ways that can change their characteristics and working properties, *for example paper to papier-mache*.
(Also applying aspects of Science ATs 6 and 11.)

Energy

- to recognise that a source of energy is needed to make a model, machine or device work;

- to use a variety of energy sources, *for example batteries, elastic bands, themselves*, and devices which transfer energy, *for example lamps, motors, sails, levers*, in experimenting and model making;

- to control, in simple ways, energy sources to meet specific needs, *for example switches in electrical circuits*;

- that forces, *such as the weight of objects used*, need to be considered when designing and making.
(Also applying aspects of Science ATs 10 and 13.)

Business and Economics

- that goods and services resulting from design and technological activities can be advertised, distributed, bought and sold;

- that within the provision of goods and services people work in teams but have specialist roles;

- that resources, *such as materials and time*, are limited and that choices must be made about their use.

Tools and Equipment

- to recognise, handle and use safely a variety of tools and equipment;

- to recognise that tools and equipment need to be safely stored and maintained;

- to use these tools and equipment to shape, cut, reform, join, mark and finish a variety of materials.

Aesthetics
- to recognise, and use the basic characteristics of line, shape, form, structure, light, colour, pattern and texture, when designing and making;

- to recognise and use basic spatial relationships, *such as elements in a pattern and parts of a machine*;

- to recognise in the made world a variety of forms resulting from people's different values and beliefs;

- to recognise the relationships between the aesthetic characteristics of an artefact or environment and how people react to those characteristics.
  (Also applying aspects of Mathematics ATs 10 and 11.)

Systems
- to identify the function performed by a system and/or sub-system within a product, *for example torch, clockwork or electrical toy*;

- to consider what is the input and output of a system, *for example a hand whisk, hand drill*;

- to consider how effective a simple system is and whether modifications could be made, *for example showing visitors around a school*;

- to give a sequence of instructions to control outcomes, including movement, *for example control a robot device or arrowhead on the screen.*
  (Also applying aspects of Science ATs 10, 11, 12 and 13.)

Structures
- that structures occur naturally or can be manufactured, *for example plant stems, honeycombs, spider's web, corrugated paper*;

- to recognise that structures have distinctive characteristics including form and stability, and to use this when creating structures, *for example pylons, puppets*;

- that structues respond to the forces applied to them, *for example placing a load on paper folded in different sections.*
  (Also applying aspects of Science AT 10.)

Mechanisms
- how mechanisms can change one type of motion to another by using interconnected parts, *for example through linkages*;

- to model simple linkage systems to achieve a desired output, *for example to make a vehicle climb a ramp.*
  (Also applying aspects of Science ATs 10, 11 and 13.)

Exploring and Investigating

- to explore needs and opportunities prior to proposing solutions;

- to gather, organise and store information, by methods including questionnaires and simple tests, which can be used as part of their designing and making.

- to appraise familiar products to see how they meet their intended use.
(Also applying aspects of Science ATs 1 and 12, Mathematics ATs 1, 9, 12 and 13, English AT 1 and 2 and Information Technology AT.)

Imaging and Generating

- to recognise that imaging can generate ideas for action;

- to use their imagination to explore ideas; by means *such as brainstorming, role play, examining objects and places, drawing and modelling.*

Modelling and Communicating

- that there is a relationship between the form and purpose of a drawing or model;

- how to develop the range of techniques they use in drawing and modelling, *such as observational drawings, annotated drawings, sketches, scale and working models, simple measurements of people and products.*
(Also applying aspects of Science ATs 12 and 13 and English ATs 1 and 3.)

Organising and Planning

- to organise their work;

- to identify what should be done;

- to take into account constraints, *such as time, availability of materials or equipment*;

- to plan a sequence to aid making.

Making

- to employ making skills safely in order to translate their designs into outcomes;

- to use tools and equipment in a proper and sensitive manner, in ways appropriate to the material being worked and to the task in hand;

- to rearrange materials during making, *for example folding, bending and mixing*;

- to make products with regard to quality;

- that holding work appropriately is essential for safe practice.

Appraising

- that appraisal should occur throughout designing and making;

● to evaluate the outcome of their work against the original intention;

● to propose simple modifications that might improve the effectiveness of their design solution;

● to reflect, individually and in groups, on how they went about designing and making and how and why they might change the procedure if they were to do it again;

● to evaluate in simple subjective ways products designed and made by others.

Health and Safety

● that at all times tools, materials and equipment should be used safely;

● to be aware of the potential dangers of the misuse of materials, tools and equipment and the health implications of such actions.
(Also applying aspects of Science AT 11.)

Social and Environmental

● that in producing a solution to a need or opportunity may well result in causing other problems;

● to recognise the social, economic and environmental effects of technological solutions.

Statements of Attainment – Level 4

AT 1 Investigate familiar contexts, and also some which require pupils to construct a working understanding of a less familiar situation (*for example a local museum, a bus station, a school kitchen*).

Devise simple ways of gathering information (*for example interview and questionnaires and simple tests*) in addition to using printed and other sources.

Recognise the points of view of others and consider what it is like to be in another person's situation.

Know that in history and in other cultures people have used design and technology to solve familiar problems (*for example providing shelter*) in many different ways.

Demonstrate that a range of criteria, sometimes conflicting (*for example costs versus safety, finish versus time available*), can be used in making judgements about what is worth doing.

Provide both oral and written justifications for the conclusions they reach as a result of their investigation of contexts.

AT 2 Record the progress of their ideas, showing how they have clarified and developed them.

Review each idea using information obtained from their own investigations and from other sources as appropriate (*for example text books, people*).

Extend their initial ideas by combining various aspects as appropriate to fomulate a design proposal (*for example by taking elements from a variety of ideas*).

Explore their design proposal in order to identify where decisions still need to be made, list these and suggest possible courses of action including modifications where appropriate which will improve their original design proposal.

Estimate the resource requirements (*for example time, materials, tools, skills*) and check on their availability.

Use drawings and models (*for example simple plans, elevations, sections, flow diagrams, patterns and templates*) and use basic editing techniques (*for example story boards, page layout*) in order to develop ideas and make modifications.

AT 3 Use their knowledge of the working characteristics (*for example flexibility, texture, colour*) of a range of readily available materials to identify those most suitable for the task in hand.

Choose tools, equipment and processes suitable for making their design and use these safely, accurately and with respect for future use.

Adopt procedures which will minimise waste (*for example in measuring out ingredients and materials*), paying regard to cost and achieve an acceptable accuracy and finish.

Adopt alternative ways of carrying forward their plan for making when they encounter obstacles, showing an awareness of when to seek help.

Use drawings, diagrams and models, as appropriate, to assist making.

Explain to others the order in which they will go about their tasks.

AT 4 Review the ways in which their design has developed during their design and technological activity, justifying their decisions and appraise outcomes in terms of original intentions.

Review the judgements they have made (*for example the choice and use of resources, the planning of their activities and aesthetic, economic considerations*) in achieving their final artefacts, systems or environments.

Comment upon existing artefacts, systems or environments, and those from other times and cultures, in terms of form and function, including appearance, use of resources.

Describe the social and economic implications of some artefacts, systems or environments (*for example, for jobs, for the quality of life*).

Programme of Study for Level 4

At Level 4 Pupils Should Develop Design and Technological Capability Through Activities:

- which each involve all the attainment targets, and which are always purposefully developed in response to perceived needs or opportunities;

- which are developed progressively to extend their experience from contexts which are familiar, to ones which are less familiar;

- some short and some extended, arising from a variety of contexts and requiring an increasing breadth of knowledge, skills and values;

- which offer increasing opportunities for them to identify their own tasks for designing and making from within given contexts;

- which involve simulations, role play, visits and visitors, *for example local businesses or service industries*;

- which introduce them to appraising the artefacts, systems or environments created by others;

- undertaken individually and in groups which develop personal qualities necessary for successful design and technological work.

To Achieve Level 4 Across the Attainment Targets Pupils Should be Taught:

Materials and Components

- to recognise the different working properties, *for example flexibility and softness*, and aesthetic characteristics of natural and manufactured materials;

- to join materials and components in both permanent and semi-permanent forms, *for example gluing and pinning*;

- to select and use materials, media and components appropriately by matching their characteristics and properties to needs when designing;

- how to rearrange materials in order to change their strength or character and to increase their usefulness when designing and making, *for example folding and bending paper, using material for hinges*.
  (Also applying aspects of Science ATs 6 and 11.)

Energy

- to recognise the energy sources in a variety of familiar devices and situations;

- to select and use a variety of energy sources, *for example batteries, elastic bands, themselves,* and devices which transfer energy, *for example lamps, motors, sails, levers,* to meet different design needs;

- to take into account the characteristics of different energy sources when designing products, *such as the weight of a battery or the variability of winds or sunlight;*

- to select and apply methods of controlling the use of energy to meet design needs, *for example switches, gears, taps, valves;*

- that there are a number of different forces *such as gravity and friction,* acting on objects, and that these need to be considered when designing and making products.
  (Also applying aspects of Science ATs 10 and 13.)

Business and Economics

- that needs and preferences of consumers influence the design and production of goods and services;

- that advertising helps promote goods and services;

- that costs include considerations of time, people, skills, money, equipment and materials;

- that products may be designed to be produced singly or in quantity and this affects what each costs.

Tools and Equipment

- to select and use the correct tools and equipment for the purpose intended;

- to check the conditions of tools and equipment to ensure they can be used efficiently, effectively and safely;

- to use tools intelligently and skilfully to produce work of appropriate quality.

Aesthetics

- to use, in combination, aesthetic characteristics of line, shape, form, structure, light, colour, pattern and texture to produce a desired effect;

- to use spatial relationships in order to create desired two and three dimensional effects;

- to design artefacts or environments in order to create aesthetic effects;

- to exploit the ways in which people react to, or might react to, aesthetic characteristics expressed through their designing and making activities.
  (Also applying aspects of Mathematics ATs 10 and 11.)

Systems

- to use their knowledge and understanding of systems and sub-systems to inform their designing and making activities;

- to consider the efficiency of a designed system in terms of inputs and outputs;

- to consider the efficiency of a system and whether design modifications should be made, in order to improve it;

- to discuss the different methods of controlling movement and effects, including the use of IT, *such as on the screen and through programmable robots*, and to use some of these different methods when designing.
  (Also applying aspects of Science ATs 10, 11, 12 and 13.)

Structures

- that a structure can be seen as a sub-set of systems;

- how structures respond to simple external forces by bending, twisting or failing at joints;

- to use their knowledge and understanding of structures to design and make a structure which will withstand a specific loading, *for example a bridge*;

- to recognise that familiar situations, *such as the organisation of a school*, can be represented by a structure.
  (Also applying aspects of Science AT 10.)

Mechanisms

- that mechanisms can be seen as a sub-set of systems;

- to select appropriate mechanisms to change one type of motion into another, *for example gears and cranks*;

- to exploit the potential of simple linkage systems when designing and modelling to achieve desired outcome;

- that mechanisms need to be controlled if they are to achieve their intended function, *for example steering a bicycle, changing gear on a bicycle or applying a brake*.
  (Also applying aspects of Science ATs 10, 11 and 13.)

Exploring and Investigating

- to explore and investigate a range of different contexts in order to identify opportunities for design and technological activities;

- to collect, refer to, and use information relevant to contexts when investigating their potential for design and technological activities;

- to propose modifications to existing products that would improve their efficacy, performance, appeal and efficiency.
  (Also applying aspects of Science ATs 1 and 12, Mathematics ATs, 1, 9, 12 and 13, English AT 1 and 2 and Information Technology AT.)

Imaging and Generating	● to recognise the necessary connection between imaging, modelling and recording when designing;
	● to generate ideas and to explore ways in which they can be further developed and refined when designing and making by means, *such as brainstorming, role play, examining objects and places, drawing and modelling.*
Modelling and Communicating	● that communication depends on a consideration of what is to be conveyed, the audience and the medium to be used;
	● to use drawings and models in order to explore ideas and make modifications, when designing and making;
	● how to extend the range of techniques in drawing and modelling, *such as simple plans, elevations, sections, pictorial perspective, flow diagrams, patterns and templates;*
	● how to plan and structure their communication through the use of basic editing techniques, *such as scripts, storyboards, page layouts and rehearsals.* (Also applying aspects of Mathematics ATs 12 and 13 and English ATs 1 and 3.)
Organising and Planning	● to plan their work carefully recognising that they may need to accommodate new ideas or opportunities as they arise when designing and making;
	● to use their knowledge and judgement to decide how to proceed in light of conflicting priorities or constraints;
	● to organise working spaces and to plan procedures and sequences for practical activities;
	● to organise teams when working as groups.
Making	● to develop their sensitivity in using tools and materials together;
	● to employ their skills safely, with increasing control when making their designs;
	● to make as appropriate two and three dimensional models of their design ideas or proposals and to test these for suitability before proceeding further;
	● to use correct procedures when working materials in order to achieve outcomes of quality;
	● to finish their work carefully, in ways that are appropriate to the task, in order to display a quality which enhances the product.

Appraising	● that evaluation is necessary at each stage of their work;
	● that making adjustments as a result of evaluation may be necessary while designing and making;
	● to evaluate with some objectivity the outcome of their design and technological activities against the original need;
	● to propose modifications that would improve the overall quality of their design outcome and its effectiveness when measured against the original intention;
	● to reflect on the approach taken, procedures adopted and outcome achieved and to relate any changes they would have made to the planning of their next task;
	● to evaluate subjectively products designed and made by others.
Health and Safety	● to be aware that a well ordered environment is essential for safe working;
	● to take some responsibility for keeping their working area orderly and safe. (Also applying apsects of Science AT 11.)
Social and Environmental	● to consider the possible consequences of their design proposals before taking them forward to completion;
	● to recognise the needs and values of groups from a variety of backgrounds and cultures when designing.

Statements of Attainment – Level 5

AT 1 Investigate contexts in a systematic way, showing judgement in the choice of sources of information and the use of both qualitative and quantitative data, as appropriate.

Recognise in their identification of needs and opportunities for design and technological activities that business considerations and the likes and dislikes of users are important.

AT 2 Record the progress of their ideas, showing how they have clarified and developed them.

Seek out information from a range of sources and organise this to help them develop their ideas and detail their design proposal.

Extend their initial ideas by combining various aspects as appropriate to formulate a design proposal and state reasons why some ideas were not used.

Specify what they intend to do and what they will need by using simple drawings, models, plans (*for example technical and symbolic representation of components*).

Establish and check the availability of the resources required (*for example time, materials, skills, tools and equipment*) adapting their design as appropriate.

AT 3 Use their knowledge of the properties and working characteristics of a range of materials and components to identify those most suitable for their design and use this knowledge while making.

Demonstrate by their choice and use of a variety of tools and equipment that they understand the basic principles upon which these work and the requirements for safety and accuracy.

Identify sub-stages in their making and co-ordinate these into a simple plan to ensure an efficient use of time, materials and labour.

Systematically apply their knowledge of materials, components and processes to overcome problems in making as these arise.

Use their knowledge of technical and symbolic representations of materials, components and processes to assist making (*for example drawings, working models, prototypes, quarter scale garment models*).

AT 4 Justify the materials, components, procedures, techniques and processes used, and indicate possible improvements.

Appraise the outcome in terms of the original needs or opportunities (*for example how well it works, convenience of use, appearance*) and how it might be improved (*for example if they were to make it again, what would they change about what they did and how they went about it*), taking into account users' views.

Understand that artefacts, systems or environments from other times and cultures have identifiable characteristics and styles, and draw upon this knowledge in their design and technological activities.

Programme of Study for Level 5

At Level 5 Pupils Should Develop Design and Technological Capability Through Activities:

- which each involve all the attainment targets, and which are always purposefully developed in response to perceived needs or opportunities;

- which have differing focuses, some demanding the need to work to a given specification, others where they develop their own task from identified needs or opportunities;

- which vary in duration, *for example six hours to twenty four hours*;

- which develop confidence in designing and making and allow them to take increasing responsibility for the form and nature of their work;

- which enable them to seek out and apply knowledge, skills and values in a constructive and purposeful manner;

- which offer increasing opportunities for them to identify their own tasks for designing and making from within given contexts;

- which introduce them to appraising the artefacts, systems or environments created by others;

- which involve simulations, visits and visitors;

- which foster enterprise and initiative;

- undertaken individually and in groups which develop personal qualities, necessary for successful design and technological work.

To Achieve Level 5 Across the Attainment Targets Pupils Should be Taught:

Materials and Components

- a working knowledge of the characteristics of a range of materials, media and components, *for example hardness, flexibility, reaction to heat and strain*;

- how to select materials and components against criteria, *such as characteristics, cost, availability and intended outcome*, when designing;

- to join materials and components in both permanent and semi-permanent forms.
  (Also applying aspects of Science ATs 6 and 11.)

Energy

- that there are various primary sources that can provide energy, *such as sun, water, wind, hot rocks, fossil and nuclear fuels;*

- that electricity provides a versatile means of transferring energy;

- that transferring and using energy results in effects, *such as heating and the generation of forces*, and that these effects need to be considered when designing and making.
  (Also applying aspects of Science ATs 10 and 13.)

Business and Economics

- to recognise the importance of consumer choice and hence the importance of product quality when designing;

- to identify markets for goods and services;

- to plan a simple budget, *for example calculating the unit costs and value added to the final product;*

- that in the production and distribution of goods and services, the control of stock is an important consideration;

- that original designs can be granted patents.
  (Also applying aspects of Mathematics ATs 1,3 and 4.)

Tools and Equipment

- to apply the appropriate techniques and processes when using tools and equipment in a safe and accurate manner;

- to recognise the purposes of a variety of tools and equipment, to understand their handling characteristics and the basic principles upon which they work, and to apply these to the task in hand.

Aesthetics

- to make the connections between aesthetic characteristics in the natural and made world and relate these to their own work;

- to use materials, processes, tools and equipment to produce specific aesthetic results;

- that appearance plays an important part in the value that consumers and users place on an artefact or an environment.
  (Also applying aspects of Mathematics ATs 10 and 11.)

Systems

- to identify systems, sub-systems, components and their functions and relationships, and use this knowledge to inform their designing and making activities;

- that all systems are subject to control in ways which involve inputs, outputs, feedback and stability.
  (Also applying aspects of Science ATs 10, 11, 12 and 13.)

Structures

- to test simple structures they have created;

- how to recognise and represent organisational structures, *for example street plans, operation of services such as police, fire or ambulance*.
  (Also applying aspects of Science AT 10.)

Mechanisms

- to identify the basic principles of a range of different mechanisms, *such as linkages and gears*, to achieve rotary, linear, oscillating and reciprocating motion and convert this from one form to another;

- to select and use simple mechanisms, including linkages and gearing, when creating prototypes and designing and making;

- to recognise the various forces which operate on and influence mechanisms, including friction and dynamic forces.
  (Also applying aspects of Science ATs 10, 11 and 13.)

Exploring and Investigating	● to be systematic in the exploration and investigation of contexts for the identification of needs and opportunities;
	● that purposeful investigation requires them to gather, select and organise data so that it can be used;
	● that exploration and investigation form a platform for the generation of ideas;
	● to investigate existing artefacts or systems or environments with a view to applying aspects in new designs. (Also applying aspects of Science ATs 1 and 12, Mathematics ATs 1, 9, 12 and 13, English ATs 1 and 2 and Information Technology AT.)
Imaging and Generating	● to break design tasks into sub-tasks and to focus on each in turn as a way of extending and developing the generation of ideas throughout designing and making.
Modelling and Communicating	● to recognise the relationship between two dimensional representations and three dimensional forms;
	● how to present their design and technological ideas and proposals using modelling techniques and specialist vocabulary, *such as conceptual drawings and models, brief writing and report writing*;
	● to develop a personal style of expression. (Also applying aspects of Mathematics ATs 12 and 13.)
Organising and Planning	● to organise and plan so that their work becomes more effective;
	● how to modify their intentions as unexpected situations arise;
	● to allocate time and other resources effectively throughout the designing and making activity.
Making	● that making requires co-ordination, control and sensitivity when using tools and equipment to work materials satisfactorily, and that it may be necessary in some cases to practise an operation in order to ensure a successful outcome;
	● to use a range of graphic techniques and processes to make, *for example packaging products and advertising products*;
	● how to achieve an acceptable minimum degree of quality in their work with respect to accuracy and finish;
	● to exercise persistence in the course of their making, as appropriate, to achieve a successful outcome;
	● how to assemble materials and components when making.

Appraising
- how to establish and apply criteria to assist their judgements about:

   the needs and opportunities identified
   the choice of materials, components, tools and equipment to achieve their design
   designing and making procedures adopted
   the outcome of their design;

- how to use their appraisal of the work of others in order to help their own design and technological activity.

Health and Safety
- to take responsibility for the working environments and ensure it is well ordered and safe;

- to identify hazards in the working environment at school;

- to take appropriate action when dangerous situations occur.

Social and Environmental
- to investigate the effects of design and technological activity on the environment;

- to consider the needs and values of individuals and of groups from a variety of backgrounds and cultures, when designing. (Also applying aspects of Science AT 16.)

Index